# KIDS' TRAVEL GUIDE TO THE ARMOR OF GOD

**Group®**

Loveland, Colorado

# Group resources actually work!

This Group resource incorporates our R.E.A.L. approach to ministry. It reinforces a growing friendship with Jesus, encourages long-term learning, and results in life transformation, because it's

**Relational**
Learner-to-learner interaction enhances learning and builds Christian friendships.

**Experiential**
What learners experience through discussion and action sticks with them up to 9 times longer than what they simply hear or read.

**Applicable**
The aim of Christian education is to equip learners to be both hearers and doers of God's Word.

**Learner-based**
Learners understand and retain more when the learning process takes into consideration how they learn best.

# Kids' Travel Guide™ to the Armor of God

Copyright © 2004 Group Publishing, Inc./0000 0001 0362 4853

Visit our website: **group.com**

## Credits
Contributing Authors: Gwyn D. Borcherding, Teryl Cartwright, Diane Cory, Jan Kershner, and Beth Robinson
Editor: Amy Nappa
Chief Creative Officer: Joani Schultz
Copy Editor: Loma Huh
Art Director: Kari Monson
Designers: Andrea Boven Nelson and Susan Tripp
Interior Illustrator: Steve Duffendack
Cover Art Director: Bambi Eitel
Cover Illustrator: Illustrated Alaskan Moose
Production Manager: Peggy Naylor

## Library of Congress Cataloging-in-Publication Data
Kids' travel guide to the armor of God.-- 1st American pbk. ed.
    p. cm.
     ISBN 978-0-7644-2695-7 (pbk. : alk. paper)
     1. Spiritual warfare--Study and teaching (Elementary) 2. Christian education of children. I. Group Publishing.
     BV4509.5.K46 2004
     268'.432--dc22                             2003025712

21       17
Printed in the United States of America.

# Table of Contents

**Introduction** 5

**Journey 1** 9

No Fear!

**Journey 2** 16

Resist!

**Journey 3** 25

What Is God's Armor?

**Journey 4** 33

Strong in the Lord

**Journey 5** 42

The Belt of Truth

**Journey 6** 50

The Breastplate of Righteousness

**Journey 7** 58

Fitted Feet

## Journey 8    65
### The Shield of Faith

## Journey 9    72
### The Helmet of Salvation

## Journey 10    80
### The Sword of the Spirit

## Journey 11    87
### The Power of Prayer

## Journey 12    93
### Stand Firm With Family and Friends

## Journey 13    101
### Standing Firm in the World

# An Introduction to the Travel Guide

**Kids' Travel Guide**

Although we can't touch or see the spiritual realm, it's as real as the rest of our world. According to the Bible, a battle rages between the spiritual followers of Satan and the followers of God. In the end we know that God will win the war, but in the meantime, our adversary, the devil, is deceiving multitudes of people, including children.

Children may imagine Satan as a red-faced and horned man wearing a pointed goatee and carrying a pitchfork. Movies and cartoons may show the devil as a hideous and frightful creature, or as a goofy fool whom a clever hero can trick. Or, to keep them from nighttime fears, kids may be told that the devil isn't real. Yet the Bible tells us that Satan is a real and powerful being who deceives, accuses, tempts, and slanders people, seeking to draw them away from God. The Bible also instructs us to guard and arm ourselves against these attacks, specifically with the armor of God.

This guidebook digs into what it means for a child to "put on" the armor of God. In an era filled with war and terrorism, children already realize there's evil in the world. The aim of this book is to help children realize they can turn to God for protection, guidance, and comfort when fears and dangers are overwhelming. Through these lessons children will discover how they can draw strength from a relationship with God.

*Kids' Travel Guide™ to the Armor of God* was designed to be applicable to kids in grades K–5. The lessons explore the power of God, the reality of the devil, and how God provides protection against the devil's attacks, as well as practical teaching on how children can stand firm in their faith.

During this thirteen-week course, each child will complete a **Travel Journal.** The Travel Journal will serve as a keepsake so that the concepts behind these lessons become written upon kids' hearts and lived out in their everyday experiences.

The **Pathway Point** is the central concept that children will explore and apply to their lives. The **In-Focus Verse** is either the Bible verse mentioning a specific part of the armor of God, or a verse that summarizes the concept behind the Pathway Point. A **Travel Itinerary** introduces the lesson and explains how the lesson will impact the lives of children.

Please read each lesson thoroughly, and make a model for the crafts before class. If you do, your lessons will flow much more smoothly. The time recommendations are only guidelines. They will change according to how many are in your group, how prepared you are, and how much help you have. Choose activities or

DEPARTURE PRAYER

TOUR GUIDE TIP

SCENIC ROUTE →

1st STOP DISCOVERY

STORY EXCURSION

ADVENTURES IN GROWING

SOUVENIRS →

HOME AGAIN PRAYER

adapt them based on the size of your group and the time you have during your class.

Each lesson starts with a **Departure Prayer.** These are creative prayer activities that help introduce the topic and focus children on God. **Tour Guide Tips** are helps for the teacher, and **Scenic Routes** provide additional creative options.

**First Stop Discoveries** introduce the children to the lesson's topic. The **Story Excursions** are Bible stories or Scripture passages that illustrate a Bible truth to support each concept. Kids will experience these stories in creative ways, and the stories will give your class variety. Choose what you think will best meet your children's needs. The activities in **Adventures in Growing** lead the children into further application of the Pathway Point. Each week, ask the children if they had opportunities to demonstrate the previous week's concept in their own lives. This will be an important faith-growing time.

**Souvenirs** are photocopiable paper activities. Have children collect these and keep them in a notebook or folder. When your study on the armor of God is complete, each child will have a Travel Journal keepsake to use as a reminder of all he or she has learned. Each lesson closes with a **Home Again Prayer**, which offers a time of commitment and a time to ask God to direct kids' lives.

Anytime during your lesson, read the **Fun Facts** section to the kids. These provide examples of the lesson's point with familiar and not-so-familiar facts.

You'll find a photocopiable handout on page 8 that shows two children in armor. Use this to make an overhead transparency that can be used during the weeks that mention specific pieces of armor. Most children will know what a sword or helmet is, but they may not be familiar with items such as a breastplate or shield. You may also want to make a copy of this page for each child to include in his or her Travel Journal.

You can add an element of fun to these lessons by dressing up in "armor" each week. Or, if you're really adventurous, you can have the kids make armor over the weeks and let them wear it as they add new pieces. Here are a few ideas:

*Belt:* Use lengths of rope as belts, or let the children braid or twist yarn into belts.

*Breastplate:* Make breastplates from craft foam or poster board and attach them to children's chests with yarn.

*Shoes:* Make simple sandals by letting children trace their feet on craft foam and then cut out the shapes. Have kids use a hole punch to make two holes along each side of each shape, then use yarn or shoelaces as the laces to hold the sandals over their feet. Or bring in all kinds of funny shoes from your house!

*Shield:* Trash can lids and the lids to large pots make fun shields. Or use large sheets of poster board cut into shield shapes. Staple shorter strips of poster board to the sides to make handles.

*Helmet:* Any kind of funny hat, from a shower cap to a football helmet, makes a fun helmet. Or stop by a local paint store and buy inexpensive painter's hats for the kids.

*Sword:* Cardboard swords covered with foil are safer than sticks or wooden swords. Or use the empty tubes from paper towels or gift wrap.

Exploring the armor of God will be a blessing to both you and the children in your class. May God bless you as you help children grow closer to God and stronger in their faith.

# No Fear!

**Pathway Point:** 🌀 God is most powerful.

**In-Focus Verse:** "Finally, be strong in the Lord and in his mighty power" (Ephesians 6:10).

## Travel Itinerary

The first step in exploring the spiritual armor God provides to believers is to acknowledge that we face spiritual enemies. Satan and the spiritual forces that fight against God are real and powerful. When we face our own inadequacy for battle, we understand our need for a Champion who will fight for us and protect us. We recognize our dependence on the armor God provides.

Talking about Satan's threats and our vulnerability can make both children and adults feel anxious. But instead of minimizing the enemy—maximize God! Vividly portray his awesome power. Help kids experience God's protective love that surrounds them. As kids trust God and learn to wear the armor he provides, they will discover that no enemy is too great for God. Celebrate with kids that the battle has already been won by Jesus!

**TOUR GUIDE TIP** The activities in this book have been designed for multi-age groups. Select from the activities, or adapt them as needed for your class.

**DEPARTURE PRAYER** (up to 5 minutes)

As kids arrive, give each one a bottle of water. These water bottles will be used several times during the lesson. Use a permanent marker to write each child's name on his or her bottle.

Gather children to sit in a circle. During your discussion, pause and encourage kids to sip water as they think of answers. You'll want kids to drink some but not all of their water.

Ask: • **What are ways water is used?**

• **Why is water so important?**

• **In what situations might water be dangerous?**

Say: **Most of the time, water is helpful. In fact, we can't live without it. But sometimes water can be dangerous. Today's story is about a time when Jesus' disciples were in real danger from water. They needed someone powerful to save them. Fold your hands around your water bottle while we pray.**

Pray: **Dear God, thank you for giving us water. You provide water**

**Items to Pack:** individual bottles of water (one per child), permanent marker

**TOUR GUIDE TIP** Give kids time to think of different ways water is used. If they need help, mention putting out fires, soaking sore feet, generating power, and for baptism.

9

for drinking, washing, playing, and watering plants. But sometimes water can be scary too, like during storms or floods. Help us trust in your great power to protect us. Amen.

Have kids take one last drink, then close bottles tightly and place them out of the way until later in the lesson.

**Items to Pack:** newsprint, markers, masking tape

## 1st STOP DISCOVERY (15 minutes) How Scared Are You?

Through this activity, children will explore diverse responses to common fears.

Before class, use newsprint and markers to make two signs. One should read "Not Scared At All!" and have a happy face. The other should read "Very Scared!" and have a sad or frightened face. Post these two signs on opposite sides of the room.

Say: **Not everyone is scared by the same things or to the same degree. We're going to do an activity to show which things are scary for us and which are not. When I read a sentence, decide if it's very scary, not scary at all, or perhaps somewhere in between.** Point out the signs and indicate where kids should stand to show different degrees of fear. Allow kids to move after each question.

Ask: • **How scared do you feel...in the dark in your room at night?**

• **How scared would God be in that situation?** Allow time for kids to move again. Include this question after each of the following questions about fears.

• **How scared would you feel...on the first day at a new school?**

• **...if your teacher called on you and you didn't know the answer?**

• **...if a strange dog approached and began to growl at you?**

• **...if you were separated from your parents in a crowded place?**

• **...if there was a severe thunderstorm while you were at home?**

• **...if there was a thunderstorm while you were in a boat on a lake?**

Gather kids together and discuss the following questions.

Ask: • **What is it about these situations that makes people feel scared?**

• **When you are scared, what do you do to feel safe again?**

• **Why isn't God afraid of anything?**

• **How can God help us when we're afraid?**

Say: **God is never afraid because he is in control; nothing can**

**TOUR GUIDE TIP**

Be sure kids don't tease others about their fears. Remind them that everyone feels afraid at times. You can promote openness by sharing something appropriate that you were afraid of as a child, or something that you're afraid of even now as an adult.

**FUN FACT**

An irrational or intense fear is called a *phobia*. It is different from ordinary fears in that the intensity of the fear is far greater than the actual danger. Some phobias have interesting names. Ereuthophobia is the fear of blushing. The fear of bees is called melisophobia. What if the disciples had cymophobia (the fear of waves) or astraphobia (the fear of lightning)?

harm him. God loves us and promises to protect us. Since  God is most powerful, we don't have to be afraid.

**STORY EXCURSION**

(15 minutes)
## Wild Wind, Wet Waves

Children will experience the wildness of a storm and the calm when Jesus showed his power.

**Items to Pack:** Bible, water bottles from the Departure Prayer, bath towels

Say: **Today's wild and wet Bible story comes from Mark 4:35-41.** Open your Bible and show children where this account is found. **Let's act out this story together and imagine what it might have been like to be on the boat with Jesus.** Ask for volunteers to play the parts of Jesus and two disciples. Have these children sit in an imaginary boat. Choose another child to turn lights on and off to imitate lightning.

Give half of the remaining children bath towels and give the other half two water bottles each. (Children do not have to have their own water bottles.) As you distribute bottles, check that the lids are on securely. Tell children to listen and act out their parts as you retell the story.

Say: **When I mention the wild wind, everyone with bath towels should flap them toward the imaginary boat carrying Jesus and the disciples. When I mention the wet waves, everyone with water bottles should shake them to make sloshing sounds.** Practice both parts with the children.

Have children re-enact the story as you read. Pause after each mention of specific actions so children have time to participate.

Say: **At the end of the day, Jesus and his disciples got into a boat to cross to the other side of the lake. Jesus lay down in one end of the boat and went right to sleep. When they were in the middle of the lake, a terrible thunderstorm came up. There was no time to get to shore. The wild wind blew the boat! The wet waves roared! Lightning flashed all around them! The disciples felt the water coming into the boat around their ankles. They thought the boat was about to sink and they would drown. They went to Jesus and woke him up. They shouted over the noise of the storm, "Jesus, don't you care if we drown?"**

**Jesus woke up and looked around at the wild wind, the wet**

**TOUR GUIDE TIP** Make sure this energetic activity remains safe. Provide enough space between kids with towels so they will not hit others. Don't allow kids to "snap" towels. Remind kids to keep water bottles tightly closed.

**SCENIC ROUTE →** Increase the fun in your storytelling by providing a few spray bottles for kids to simulate rain and mist!

waves and the crashing lightning. He stood up. He calmly said, "Quiet, waves." Then he said, "Hush, wind." The lightning stopped. Suddenly everything became completely still.

**Let's imitate how quiet the lake was.** Wait for children to settle. **Let's get quieter still.** Pause, then whisper: **Let's listen to that silence for ten seconds.** Wait, then continue in a whisper. **The disciples looked at the quiet lake. They looked at Jesus. They looked at each other and said, "Jesus stopped a storm! He's someone special!"**

**The disciples were right. Jesus *is* someone special. Jesus is God. Since  God is most powerful, we don't have to be afraid.**

Gather kids together and lay props aside. Have kids form pairs to discuss the following questions. After kids share with each other, ask for volunteers to share their answers with the group.

Ask: • **What would you have thought if you were in the boat with Jesus when the lake became quiet?**

• **How do you think the disciples felt when they realized that Jesus was so powerful?**

• **How do you feel knowing that  God is most powerful?**

• **How do you need God's power in your life?**

Say: **Jesus showed his power and protected his friends by calming the storm. God is still able to protect us today. One way God protects us from spiritual enemies is by giving us spiritual armor. We're going to be learning about the armor of God in the coming weeks. We'll discover that whatever problems or enemies we face,  God is most powerful.**

**Items to Pack:** tennis balls, masking tape, markers, newsprint

**ADVENTURES IN GROWING**

(up to 10 minutes)
## The Fear Zone

Kids will play a game to discover that fears can be difficult to stop on our own.

Use two strips of masking tape to mark three playing areas as shown on page 13. Clear the playing area of any obstacles.

Work with the children to create a list of things kids fear. Write these ideas on newsprint, then post this where kids can easily see it.

Have children form two teams, the Rollers and the Defenders. Have the Rollers stand in section A and the Defenders stand in section B.

Say: **We've talked about common fears. Now let's play a game to** see how well we're able to stop those fears. The Rollers will call out a fear from our list, then roll a ball toward the Defenders. The balls must stay on the floor, but the Rollers can have as many balls in play at a time as they like.

Defenders will stand behind their line and try to keep the balls from getting past them and into the Fear Zone. Balls can be stopped only with your hands, and they must be gently rolled back to the Rollers. If a ball gets into the Fear Zone, it has to stay there and can't be returned to the game.

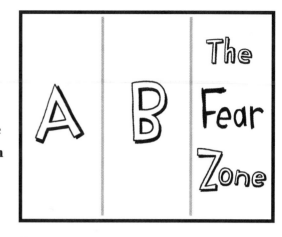

Begin the game. Encourage kids to play quickly, rolling balls as soon as they are returned. After several minutes, have teams switch roles and play again.

Gather kids together to discuss the game.

Ask: • **How successful were you at stopping the fears that came your way?**

• **What made it hard or easy to stop the fears?**

• **In real life, is it hard or easy to stop yourself from having fears? Why?**

• **Ephesians 6:10 says, "Finally, be strong in the Lord and in his mighty power." How can God's power help us be strong enough to face our fears?**

• **What fears do you need strength to face?**

Say: **Even though some of the fears got past these Defenders, nothing can get past God. No matter what the problem, we don't have to be afraid because  God is most powerful.**

 (10 minutes)
## Calming the Sea

Kids will begin their Travel Journals and consider how God's power can help them face their fears.

Distribute one pocket folder to each child, and have kids write their names on the front with markers. These folders will serve as kids' Travel Journals to collect the Souvenirs activity in each lesson. Kids will take their Journals and Souvenirs home after Journey 13 as keepsakes to remind them about the armor of God.

Give each child a copy of the handout. Show kids how to fold the left edge of the page toward the center on the dotted line, concealing Jesus. With the page closed, have kids finish the left half of the boat and decorate the left flap to look like the boat is in the middle of a storm. Have the kids draw themselves in the right-hand side of the boat.

TOUR GUIDE TIP — Remind kids of these safety rules: Balls must be rolled on the floor. Defenders should return the balls to the Rollers by rolling them along the sides of the playing area.

**Items to Pack:** pocket folders (one per child), pencils, copies of the "Calming the Sea" handout (p. 15), markers

**SCENIC ROUTE** → Provide additional art supplies for children to use in decorating their pictures. Let kids use stickers, cotton balls, fish crackers, glitter, and glue to enhance their projects.

**Items to Pack:** water bottles from the Departure Prayer activity

**FUN FACT** Between 1992 and 2002, per capita bottled water consumption in the United States more than doubled, from 9.8 gallons to 21.5 gallons per year!

Then have kids open the page, revealing Jesus in the boat. On the left side of this boat, kids can add details showing the quiet lake. Have an older child read the In-Focus Verse, "Finally, be strong in the Lord and in his mighty power" (Ephesians 6:10). As children finish, have them form pairs and practice retelling the story to each other.

Ask: • **Why do you think Jesus calmed the storm for the disciples?**

• **What did the disciples learn about Jesus?**

• **What "stormy" situations have happened in your life?**

• **How can trusting Jesus help you during stormy times?**

Say: **Jesus calmed the storm and did other miracles so his disciples would know that ◕ God is most powerful. Nothing is bigger or stronger than he is. Since we belong to him, we don't have to be afraid. Even if God doesn't make our difficulties disappear, he promises to be with us through them. As we trust in him, he will give us the strength we need.**

Have children place their pictures in their Travel Journals.

**HOME AGAIN PRAYER** (10 minutes)

Have children find their water bottles and sit in a circle.

Say: **Today we learned how powerful God is. No matter what happens, he is able to protect us. Turn to a friend and tell about a stormy time in your life. Shake your water bottle to show how shook up you felt at that time.** Give kids time to share.

**As we pray, we'll talk to God about stormy times and quiet times. When we pray about stormy times, shake your water bottle. When we pray about calm times, hold your bottle so the water becomes very still.**

Pray: **Dear God, during the storm the disciples were frightened. They thought the boat might sink. They called to Jesus for help. He calmed the storm and kept them safe. Sometimes we are scared too. When we're afraid, our fears shake us up. Help us remember that ◕ you are most powerful. Help us trust you to protect us, calm us, and bring us peace. Amen.**

Let children take their water bottles home with them.

# Calming the Sea

"Finally, be strong in the Lord and in his mighty power" (EPHESIANS 6:10).

# Resist!

**Pathway Point:**  We can resist temptation.

**In-Focus Verse:** "Resist the devil, and he will flee from you" (James 4:7b).

## Travel Itinerary

The existence of Satan, or the devil, is a subject sometimes overlooked in modern ministry, and especially in children's ministry. No one wants to scare children and fill their minds with fears. In school or in other arenas outside of church, children may hear that Satan is an imaginary or mythical being. Satan is a subject we instinctively shun.

But in doing so, we do children a disservice. Satan is alive and active in the world—even in the world of children. We owe it to kids to explain his existence and his methods. Use this lesson to give your students the tools they need to resist Satan when he tempts them. Show kids that Jesus himself was tempted but didn't sin, and let kids know that they can follow Jesus' example.

Most of all, we owe it to kids to explain Satan's defeat, which was accomplished for us on the cross. Use this lesson also to reassure kids that when Jesus died on the cross for our sins, and then rose from the dead in glory, the ultimate battle against evil was won.

**DEPARTURE PRAYER** (up to 5 minutes)

Gather kids together in a circle on the floor.

Say: **Today we're learning that**  **we can resist temptation. Let's talk for a minute about what it means to resist something or someone. Find a partner and sit cross-legged across from him or her.** Pause.

**Hold your hands up in front of you and place your palms on your partner's palms. When I give the signal, gently push against your partner's palms. Try to resist your partner's pushing. But remember, no rough stuff!**

Give the signal and let partners push against each other's hands. Remind kids not to push too hard. After about thirty seconds, call time.

Ask: • **What was it like to push against your partner's hands?**

• **What would have happened if you had let up your pressure?**

• **How was having your partner push at you like being tempted to do something wrong?**

TOUR GUIDE TIP

The activities in this book have been designed for multi-age groups. Select from the activities, or adapt them as needed for your class.

TOUR GUIDE TIP

If you have an uneven number of students in class, let three kids form a trio, or be a partner yourself!

Say: **Being tempted to do wrong is a lot like being pushed in the wrong direction. But just as you pushed back against your partner's hands, you can push back against temptation. That's what it means to resist—it's like pushing back.** 🌀 **We can resist temptation.** Have kids sit in a circle.

**Think of something wrong you've been tempted to do. You won't have to tell anyone if you'd rather not. Maybe you resisted that temptation, maybe you didn't. That's not the point right now. We're all tempted, and we all sin. Raise your hand when you've thought of a temptation.** Pause.

**We're going to go around the circle in this prayer, each of us asking God to help us with our temptations. I'll start by asking God to help me resist my temptation. Then I'll take the hand of the person next to me, and instead of pushing against it I'll give it a gentle squeeze. That's to show that we can help each other resist temptation. Then that person will pray and take the next person's hand, and so on. If you feel comfortable, you can name the temptation you thought of. If not, it's perfectly OK to just say, "Please help me with my temptation." Ready? Let's pray.**

Begin the prayer by saying something like, "Dear God, please help me resist the temptation to gossip." Then take the hand of the person next to you and gently squeeze it. Go around the circle until everyone has prayed, then end the prayer by thanking God for helping us resist temptation.

### 1st STOP DISCOVERY (20 minutes) Too Many Temptations!

In this activity, kids will play a game where they'll be bombarded with all kinds of temptations.

**Items to Pack:** paper scraps, pencils

Set out pencils and a large supply of paper scraps.

Say: **On each paper scrap, write one temptation that someone your age faces. Maybe you'll write "cheating on a test," "talking back," or "hitting my sister." Think of as many temptations as you can, and write each one on a separate scrap of paper.** Give kids a minute or two to write.

**OK, now I need a brave volunteer.** Choose a volunteer to stand next to you. Have the rest of the kids form two lines facing each other, leaving an aisle in the middle. Explain that as the volunteer slowly walks down the aisle between the two rows, the rest of the class will shout out what's written on each paper scrap, as if attacking him or her with temptations.

Play several times, choosing a new volunteer for each round. Then have kids sit down.

Ask: • **When do you feel like you're being bombarded with temptations?**

• **How does this game remind you of those attacks?**

Say: **Satan is always on the lookout for ways to make us stumble and sin. He bombards us with temptations! Sometimes he tempts us to** *do* **something wrong. Other times, he tempts us to think or feel something wrong. Sometimes he appeals to our emotions, like pride or envy. Maybe you got a better grade at school than your friend and you start to think you're a better person. Or maybe your friend got a new video game and you're mad because you wanted to get it first. Or maybe you're tempted to be angry with someone. Write those types of "feeling" temptations on some more paper scraps.**

Play the game again with a new volunteer or two. Then have kids sit again.

Say: **Whew! These temptations seem overpowering! But we're not through yet. I can think of** *another* **way Satan tempts us. This time it's by tempting us to doubt God. Sometimes things happen in our lives that are hard to deal with. During hard times, it's easy to think that maybe God doesn't care about us anymore. Satan just** *loves* **to use that temptation! Anytime we're tempted to doubt God's love for us, that's the devil at work.**

**On a scrap of paper, write a word or two to describe a time you doubted God. You won't have to say it out loud if you don't want to. For example, you might write "when my Mom was sick" or "when my parents were arguing."**

Give kids a minute to write, then choose a new volunteer and play the game again with the new temptations. Then have kids sit down.

Ask: • **How can we resist these temptations that are being put in front of us all the time?**

Say: **You won't believe it, but I can think of yet** *another* **way Satan tempts us! He uses lots of tricks against us, doesn't he? This next kind of temptation is about doubt again, but this time it's about doubting ourselves. You know the kind of thoughts I mean: I'm stupid. I'm ugly. No one likes me. I'll never be good at anything.**

▲ **TOUR GUIDE TIP**

Be prepared to help kids if they're having trouble verbalizing "feeling" temptations. You could write several common ones, such as anger, pride, envy, and jealousy on a chalkboard or newsprint for kids to copy. Or you could just have kids draw faces that depict the feelings they think of.

Do you think those thoughts come from God? No way! God *loves* us. In fact, he loves us so much that he sent his only Son to die on the cross for us. He doesn't want us to think bad things about ourselves. But Satan does.

Ask: • **How do you feel when those kinds of negative thoughts go through your head?**

• **How do you treat other people when you're feeling bad about yourself?**

Say: **When we're busy feeling bad about ourselves, we're not helping other people. We're not being joyful. We're not doing the things God has ready for us to do.**

**Now don't get me wrong. Sometimes we *should* feel bad about ourselves. When we sin, the Holy Spirit will prompt us to repent and ask God to forgive us. That's a good thing.**

**But God would never tell us we're too short or too dumb or too goofy-looking. Those thoughts come from the great liar, which is what Satan is sometimes called. On these last paper scraps, write some of the bad thoughts people sometimes think about themselves.**

Give kids another few minutes to write, then choose a last volunteer and play again. After the game, have kids collect the papers and place them in a pile for use later in the lesson.

Say: **Satan tempts us in lots of ways. But we never have to feel singled out or like we're the only one he's tempting. Every person who has ever lived on this earth has been tempted. But only *one* person was tempted and never sinned. And how he handled his temptation can help us handle ours. Let's look right now at the story of how Satan tempted Jesus, and see how this teaches us that  we can resist temptation.**

**STORY EXCURSION**

(15 minutes)
## Jesus, Our Example

This activity will teach kids that even though Jesus was tempted, he never sinned. Discovering how Jesus resisted temptations will help kids resist their own.

Have kids form trios and give each trio a Bible.

Say: **Jesus was tempted three times by the devil, and each temptation was a little different. Let's look at the first temptation.** Have kids read Matthew 4:1-4 in their groups.

**SCENIC ROUTE →** This section of the activity may bring out some surprising emotions in kids. Be prepared to stop and talk in greater depth about negative thoughts if kids seem willing. Also offer to talk after class with any child who may be struggling with hard-to-handle negative thoughts. Kids may never have realized that some of the negative things they think about themselves just aren't true.

**Items to Pack:** Bibles, poster board, tape, grocery advertisements, scissors, pencils, paper, a plate of cookies (for optional Scenic Route)

SCENIC
ROUTE
→
Bring in the plate of cookies. Show the cookies to each trio, playing up how good the cookies taste and how yummy they are, to give them the idea of physical temptations. Don't let kids take any cookies until the discussion time.

FUN
FACT

Is food tempting to you? Food companies spend $30 billion a year to try to convince you to eat their foods—and to eat more of it!

Say: **Imagine if you hadn't eaten for forty days! How good food would sound. We can't even *imagine* what it would be like not to eat for forty days!**

Give each trio a sheet of poster board, scissors, tape, and some of the grocery advertisements you brought. Tell kids to cut out a picture of every food item they remember eating in the last forty days. (Round it down to a month if that's easier for kids to visualize.) Have groups tape the pictures to the poster board to form food collages. When groups have finished, hang the posters next to each other on a wall.

Say: **Look at all that food! We've eaten a lot in the last forty days. But look what Jesus ate.** Hang a blank sheet of poster board next to the collages. **He must have been starving! The idea of nourishing, fresh bread must have been tempting. Jesus certainly *could* have turned the stones into bread. It must have been tempting to show the devil that he could do it. But Jesus resisted the devil. He knew that relying on God was more important than food.**

**Now let's look at the second temptation.** Have trios read Matthew 4:5-7.

Ask: • **What do you think this temptation is all about?**

• **Why do you think Jesus answered the devil the way he did?**

• **What does it mean to "test God"?**

• **When are times you might think about testing God?**

Say: **We might think about testing God when we're feeling insecure or lonely. It might be almost like a dare. For example, maybe we're going through a hard time and we feel like God doesn't care. So maybe we say to God, "I'm angry and I don't think you care. If you care, I expect you to do such and such." It would be like a test for God to prove himself.**

**But we shouldn't test God. It's great to talk to him and tell him how we're feeling, even if we're feeling upset. It's OK to pour our hearts out to God. Just read Psalm 22 to see how even David cried out to God. But he didn't test God.**

**Now let's look at the last temptation.** Have kids read Matthew 4:8-11 in their groups.

**This temptation is pretty straightforward. Satan was offering Jesus all the power and riches in the world, if he would just worship the devil. We might not think we ever face this temptation. But when we turn away from God and put our energy and thoughts and**

time into some material thing, it's like we're worshipping that thing instead of God. And that's just what the devil wants.

In your group, think of ten material things that tempt kids your age to look away or move away from God. Write your Top 10 List to share with the rest of the class.

Give each group a pencil and a sheet of paper. Have group members work together to create their lists. After a few minutes, let each group share its list with the rest of the class.

Say: **We need to resist the temptation to let anything come between us and God.**

Ask: • **Why do you think Jesus was tempted? After all, he's God.**

• **What do you notice about how Jesus reacted to each temptation?**

Say: **It's interesting to see that Jesus used Scripture to resist each temptation. In a few minutes we'll look at some verses that can help us resist temptation. But first, let's practice a little resisting.**

Be ready to help groups with their lists as necessary, but try not to supply answers. Ask open-ended questions such as, "What things do you spend a lot of time wishing you had?" and "Are there things you have or do that you don't think God would approve of? Why?"

**ADVENTURES IN GROWING**

(10 minutes)
## Say It in Circles

This activity will help kids recognize specific temptations and think about how to resist them.

Say: **The Bible tells us in James 4:7, "Resist the devil, and he will flee from you." Let's do an activity to help us think of ways to resist the devil and his temptations.**

Have kids form pairs, and give each child paper and a pencil. On the papers, have students write as many temptations that kids face as they can think of. Remind kids of the three kinds of temptations Jesus faced: physical, testing God, and worshipping something or someone other than God. Encourage partners to brainstorm with each other.

After a few minutes, have kids form two circles, one facing out and one facing in. Kids should stand facing their partners and put their hands out, palms out, as they did in the opening prayer. Explain that at your signal, the partner in the inner circle should share one of the temptations from his or her paper. Then the children will gently press against each other's hands to demonstrate resistance as the second partner says how to resist that temptation. Encourage kids to think about what advice the Bible gives as they think how to resist.

Then everyone will take a step to the right to form new pairs. The partner in the outer circle will read a temptation and the other partners will say how to

**Items to Pack:** paper, pencils

resist. Continue play until kids get back to their original partners or until they run out of temptations. Then have kids sit down.

Say: **Just as in this game we faced one temptation after another, temptations come at us all the time in real life. We have to be on our guard so that  we can resist temptation. One way to do that is to become familiar with what the Bible says. After all, Jesus used Scripture to resist each of his temptations!**

**Items to Pack:** Bibles, copies of "Just Say No!" handout (p. 24), pens and pencils

| SOUVENIRS → | (10 minutes) |

### Just Say No!

This activity will provide a tangible resource of Bible verses that kids can turn to as they try to resist temptation.

Give each child a copy of the "Just Say No!" handout. Set out Bibles, pens and pencils for kids to use. Have children follow the directions on the handout. Kids will research and fill in the handout with verses that are meaningful to them. There are several verses provided on the handout, but you may want to suggest other verses that would be meaningful to the children, or remind them of other verses they've learned and how these might be helpful in resisting temptation.

Then have kids form pairs and let partners read their verses to each other as reinforcement. If you have time, invite volunteers to share their answers with the rest of the class.

Say: **Add these pages to your Travel Journal to remind you that the Bible will always help you resist temptation. Anytime you're not sure if something's right or wrong, or you're not sure if you're strong enough to resist a temptation, read the verses you wrote. God will help you! Let's thank God for being there for us when we face temptations, and for providing an example of how to resist.**

(10 minutes)
# Give Your Temptations to Jesus

Use this activity to demonstrate that Jesus can help us with all of our temptations.

**Items to Pack:**

temptations from opening activity, newsprint, marker, tape

Bring out the temptations written on slips of paper that you used in the 1st Stop Discovery activity. Hang a sheet of newsprint on the wall, and draw a large cross on the newsprint.

Say: **Jesus was human and he faced the same temptations we do. But he is also God, so he was the only person never to give in to temptation and sin. We can always look to his example when we're struggling with temptation.**

Explain that kids should take turns placing the paper temptations on the floor at the base of the cross you drew. Then gather kids in a semicircle near the pile of papers, and lead kids in a closing prayer. Thank Jesus for showing us the way to resist temptation and ask him to help each person in your class resist temptation during the following week.

*"Watch and pray so that you will not fall into temptation"* (MATTHEW 26:41a).

# Just Say No!

## "Resist the devil, and he will flee from you" (JAMES 4:7b).

**Directions:** Inside each circle, write a temptation that you have trouble resisting. Then under that circle, write a Bible verse that can help you resist.

*"No temptation has seized you except what is common to man. And God is faithful; he will not let you be tempted beyond what you can bear. But when you are tempted, he will also provide a way out so that you can stand up under it"* (1 CORINTHIANS 10:13).

**TEMPTATION**

*"Trust in the Lord with all your heart and lean not on your own understanding; in all your ways acknowledge him, and he will make your paths straight"* (PROVERBS 3:5-6).

## We can resist temptation.

# What Is God's Armor?

**Pathway Point:** 🌐 God's armor frees us.

**In-Focus Verse:** "So let us put aside the deeds of darkness and put on the armor of light" (Romans 13:12b).

## Travel Itinerary

In previous journeys children have considered the power of God and the power of Satan. While it's certain that God has the ultimate authority over the devil, the Bible does caution Christians to avoid evil and its temptations. In Romans 13, Paul guides readers to "put aside the deeds of darkness and put on the armor of light." Clearly, protection is needed against the forces of the devil.

When a soldier wears armor, the soldier is able to focus less on protecting himself and more on the attack. In the same way, as we put our faith into spiritual armor, we can be freed from worries and fears and instead focus on reaching out to those still in darkness.

This journey will help children realize why spiritual armor is needed, and what it means to choose God's armor, the armor of light. As children consider their need to be protected, let them know that as they stand behind the protection of God they can be freed.

**TOUR GUIDE TIP** The activities in this book have been designed for multi-age groups. Select from the activities, or adapt them as needed for your class.

**TOUR GUIDE TIP** Be aware of how the imagery of war can affect kids—especially if they are worried about family members who are deployed in the military. Emphasize that we're on a mission in which God directs us to help others, not hurt them.

**Items to Pack:** flashlight with batteries

**DEPARTURE PRAYER** (up to 5 minutes)

Have children sit in a circle. Then darken the room as much as possible.

Ask: • **How does the darkness make you feel?**

• **What are problems with darkness?**

• **How would you feel if you were in a super-dark and scary place, and then you were surrounded by light?**

Say: **When darkness is around us, we can't see the things that might trip us or we can't see dangers around us. This makes many of us feel afraid in the dark and comforted by the light. Let's share our fears with God in prayer. As each of you takes a turn praying, I'm going to shine a light over your head. This light will remind us that when we're surrounded by God we don't have to be afraid—it's like being surrounded by armor made from light.**

Stand and turn on the flashlight. Shine the light down over your own head as you pray a sentence telling God a fear. Then stand behind a child and shine the light down upon his or her head while this child prays. Move silently around the circle, shining the light on each child. If a child is uncomfortable praying aloud, let the child pray silently as you shine the light above him or her.

## Invisible Armor (up to 15 minutes)

This experiment illustrates the importance of having armor.

Give each child a paper towel, a pen or pencil, and a plastic foam cup.

Say: **Think of a few things or people that are very important to you. Write or draw these on your paper towel.**

Allow time for children to do this, then ask:

• **What kind of protection is needed for these people or things?**

• **What would you do to protect these things or people?**

• **How can these things or people be protected without your help?**

Have children crumple their paper towels into tight wads and press them firmly into the bottom of their cups. The paper towel should stay in the bottom of the cup when the cup is turned upside down.

Let each child turn his or her cup upside down, push the cup *straight* down into the water, and then pull the cup straight up and out of the water. When each child has done this, let children remove their paper towels from their cups and see if they are wet or dry. If the activity was done correctly, the paper will be dry.

If you have more than 15 children in your group, provide two or more buckets of water.

Ask: • **Why didn't your paper get wet?**

• **What protected these things that were important to you?**

Say: **A pocket of air was trapped between your paper towel and the water. The air, even though it was invisible, protected your paper towel from the water. This invisible protection of air reminds me of the invisible protection that God offers us. It's called the armor of God, and we're going to be learning more about this armor over the next few weeks.**

Ask: • **What does armor do?**

• **Who needs armor?**

• **Why would you need armor?**

Say: **Most kids don't need to wear armor like a soldier would wear. Imagine going to school each day wearing a helmet and carrying a shield. People might think you were crazy! But we do need to protect ourselves against temptation, and mean thoughts, and unkind words** and actions. For this we need God's armor. When a soldier wears armor, that soldier feels secure and safe. In the same way, when we wear the armor of God we can feel safe and secure. ◗ God's armor frees us from fear.

Ask: • **Why do you think God wants to protect you?**

• **What are things you want God to protect you from?**

• **What kind of armor do you think God might give us?**

Say: **We'll be examining the individual pieces of armor God provides in upcoming lessons. For right now, let's explore a Bible account of a time when God protected his people, freeing them from the fear of being captured by enemies.**

## STORY EXCURSION

(15 minutes)
## God's Army

Children will interact with the Bible account of Elisha and the Arameans.

**Items to Pack:** 1 red and 1 green construction paper strip per child, Bible

Say: **The Bible tells us in 2 Kings 6:8-23 about an unusual battle.**

Open your Bible and show children where this historical account is recorded in the Old Testament. Then give each child one red and one green strip of paper. Explain that these are flags kids will use as you tell the story.

Say: **I'm going to let you guess what happens next in the story as I tell it to you. Sometimes the people in the story will have the option of going ahead or moving forward. If you think they should move ahead, wave your green flag. Green means go. If you think they should stop or go back, wave your red flag. Red means stop.** Practice for a moment, calling out "Go" and "Stop" to see if kids wave the correct flag. Then continue with the Bible story.

**The king of Aram was fighting against God's people, the Israelites. He set a trap for the Israelite army by sending his army to camp in a certain location. If you were in the Israelite army, what would you do? Go forward, go backwards or stop where you are?** Give kids a moment to wave their flags and ask a few of them why they made that choice.

**There was a man named Elisha, who was a prophet of God. This means that he gave the people messages from God. God let Elisha know where the Arameans were hiding. Elisha told the king of Israel about the trap so that the Israelite army wouldn't go there. The king**

of Israel checked out what Elisha said and found out it was true! So he followed Elisha's suggestion, and the Israelites were safe. This happened so many times that the king of Aram thought one of his own men was leaking information to the Israelites. Finally he found out that Elisha was the one telling the Israelite army his plans to ambush them. The king of Aram decided to capture Elisha in the city of Dothan. If you were Elisha, what would you do? **Stay in Dothan?** (Red flag.) **Run away?** (Green flag.) Give kids a chance to wave their flags and discuss their choices.

The Aramean army surrounded Elisha. Elisha's servant asked him, "Oh Lord, what should we do?" What would you do? Go forward toward the army? Or stop and run away while you can? Let them wave their flags.

Elisha told his servant not to be afraid. He prayed that the servant might see that God's army was greater than the Aramean army. God opened the servant's eyes to see horses and chariots of fire around Elisha! What would you do now? Give kids a moment to choose a flag to wave and talk about why they picked the flag they did.

Elisha prayed that the Aramean army couldn't see and God answered his prayer by making the army blind! If you were Elisha, what would you do now? Let children wave their flags.

Elisha went up to the blind Aramean army and told them they were in the wrong place and that he would take them where they needed to go. He led the blind army straight to the king of Israel. The king of Israel was delighted and surprised to see Elisha leading the blind Aramean army right to him.

"What should I do?" The king asked Elisha. What would you do if you were the king? Wave red for put them all in prison and green to let them go. Let kids wave their flags and discuss what the king should do.

"Do not kill them," Elisha replied. "Feed them a great feast and then let them go home." The king of Israel did this, and the army of Aram stopped raiding Israel. The Israelites could now be free from the worries and fears of being attacked.

Have children put away their flags. Then ask:

• **What was surprising about this story?**

• **Why do you think the Arameans were fed and then sent home instead of being killed?**

Say: **God chose to fight differently than we might expect. God didn't want to hurt the Arameans. Instead, he wanted to show his power and protect the people of Israel.**

Ask: • **How do you think Elisha felt when he knew he was surrounded by the enemy?**

• **How do you think Elisha's servant felt?**

• **Why did Elisha feel differently than his servant? What did he know that kept him from being afraid?**

Say: **God was protecting Elisha the entire time. God let Elisha's servant see that an army of fire—an army of light—protected them. This protection allowed these men to be free from fear. God protects us too, even when we don't see him shielding us. God protects us with his armor because he loves us.** 🌀 **God's armor frees us from fears and worries.**

**ADVENTURES IN GROWING**

(up to 10 minutes)
## Armor of Light

Children will play a game to help them consider times they need God's protection.

Say: **Romans 13:12 says, "So let us put aside the deeds of darkness and put on the armor of light." This means that we should stop doing things that lead us away from God, and instead put on the armor of God. This armor protects us and frees us from worries and fear and helps us do what God wants us to do. Let's play a game to help us think about this verse and what it means for our lives.**

Have children sit in circles of about ten players. Give one child in each circle a flashlight and ask children to leave the light turned off. Explain that kids will be playing a game similar to Hot Potato. As you start the music, kids will pass the flashlight. When you stop the music, the child holding the flashlight will finish the sentence, "I need God's protection when _____." Then the child should turn on the flashlight, shine it on a different student, and this student will say, "God's armor of light can protect you and free you." Then the light should be turned off and the game begun again.

Begin the music and stop it randomly. When you stop the music, remind children of the actions to be completed, then allow a minute for answers to be shared. Begin the music and continue the game. Play until each child has had a chance to complete the sentence at least once, or as time allows. Put away the supplies.

**FUN FACT**
Armor needs to be lightweight so it doesn't hinder the soldier wearing it. If armor is too heavy, a soldier can't move quickly or defend himself very well. As you read Romans 13:12b, consider that there's an extra meaning here—not only is God's armor the armor of light, it's *light* armor!

**Items to Pack:** 1 flashlight with batteries per 10 children, radio or CD player and CD

**FUN FACT**
Even though most armor is used to defend the soldier, the sword and shoes are used to attack and defeat the enemy. The footwear of the Roman soldier was very important, because these shoes helped the soldier stand fast or move forward as he was ordered. The first "cleats" were actually worn on the battle sandals of the Roman soldiers.

**SOUVENIRS** (up to 5 minutes)
## Soldier of Light

Children will create an optical illusion to add to their Travel Journals.

Give each child a handout and a black crayon. Have the kids trace the soldier in black crayon several times, while pressing firmly with the crayon.

When kids have done this, ask them to stare intently at their finished pictures as you time them for one minute. When the minute is up, tell kids to look away from the paper and to focus on a blank wall or to turn their papers over and look at the blank side. Children will experience an optical illusion that causes the eye to momentarily see a yellow, glowing image of the same soldier that they have colored in black.

Say: **A glowing soldier has appeared instead of the soldier you colored. This soldier is wearing the bright armor of light, instead of the dark armor of the first soldier. Just like the army Elisha's servant saw, you can now see your soldier has put on the armor of light. This optical illusion is a fun way for us to begin thinking about the armor of God. ◐ God's armor frees us and protects us.**

Have children put their soldier pictures into their Travel Journals.

**SCENIC ROUTE** → Throughout history, symbols and colors have been used to identify different armies or warriors. Let children consider symbols or colors that they think represent God or the battle between good and evil. Have kids draw these symbols around the soldier on their handout. Allow time for children to share what these symbols mean to them.

**HOME AGAIN PRAYER** (up to 5 minutes)
## Protection Prayer

Say: **Let's use motions that are used in self-defense as we pray and ask God for his protection.**

Before you pray, review these motions with the children.

*Shield:* Place your arms over your chest in an X.

*Protect*: Have children place one arm at an angle over their heads as if protecting their heads from a blow.

*Block:* Have children swiftly move left hand in an angle from the right shoulder to the left side as if pushing aside or deflecting a punch.

Most of us know that animals such as crabs and armadillos use protective armor. But did you know that plants use armor too? Some plants such as peanuts and walnuts have shells to protect their seeds. Cacti have spikes to protect them, and other plants have tiny thorns on their seeds so the seeds can hitch a ride on animals and move far away from the parent plant. Now that's a creative use of armor!

When children have mastered these motions, lead them in prayer. Do the motions with them at the appropriate times.

Pray: **Lord, please use your love to shield** (shield motion) **us from things that will hurt us. Protect** (protect motion) **us from our fears and from things that take us away from you. Block** (block motion) **the efforts of those who want to hurt us, tempt us, and harm us. In Jesus' name, amen.**

# Soldier of Light

"So let us put aside the deeds of darkness and put on the armor of light"
(ROMANS 13:12b).

# JOURNEY 4

# Strong in the Lord

**Pathway Point:**  We can be strong because our power comes from God.

**In-Focus Verse:** "Finally, be strong in the Lord and in his mighty power" (Ephesians 6:10).

## Travel Itinerary

When asked to describe strength, most people think of powerful muscles and physical stamina. To be strong is equated with having bodily strength and self-reliance. But the Bible describes another kind of strength—spiritual strength that comes through faith in God. Paul's call to be strong in Ephesians 6:10 is not a cry to go into battle with physical weapons, but to rely on God's strength. The armor of God is strong because God is strong, and we are to put our trust in his invincible power instead of our own.

Trusting in God's strength rather than our own can be hard to do. We usually try to solve our problems through our own means instead of turning to God. Use this lesson to guide children to the true source of strength for every crisis—God.

**DEPARTURE PRAYER** (up to 5 minutes)

Have children form pairs. Ask one child in each pair to form fists and press these together as shown. Tell the second child in each pair to try to pull the fists of the first child apart. After several tries, let children switch roles.

Say: **This exercise makes us feel strong, but in reality, our power comes from God. Let's thank God that**  **we can be strong because our power comes from God.**

Have all the children press their fists together as you pray: **God, we know that our strength is nothing compared to yours. You are able to do more with one finger than we could ever do all together. You are able to do remarkable things, and we ask that you make us strong to do remarkable things for you too. We praise you for the strength you give us and ask that we may learn how to use your power to help lift others up into your presence.**  **We can be strong because our power comes from you. Amen.**

**TOUR GUIDE TIP**
The activities in this book have been designed for multi-age groups. Select from the activities, or adapt them as needed for your class.

**TOUR GUIDE TIP**
At this age, students may be self-conscious about their own physical strength. The stronger kids may want to show off by arm wrestling, seeing who can lift whom, or challenging you to do a feat that they can do. These activities often put others at a noticeable disadvantage. Remember to emphasize the fact that physical strength is not enough to conquer every problem.

**SCENIC ROUTE →**
Have people from your church share with your class personal stories of how they've experienced God's power in their lives. These may be "warriors of faith" who have been through physical challenges or people who can relate to situations with which your students may be struggling. Ask these volunteers to share with your kids how they stay strong in the Lord. Give kids time to ask these guests questions as well.

## STOP 1st DISCOVERY (10 minutes) Strong Breath

This experiment reminds kids that human strength has its limits.

Ask: • **Do you think you're strong? Why or why not?**

Say: **We're going to do an experiment to see how strong our lungs are.**

Have each child create a cone shape from a sheet of paper. They can do this easily by rolling a sheet of paper into a telescope shape, then twisting one end tighter than the other so that the paper looks more like a funnel. Provide tape so children may secure their paper into this shape.

Have children form pairs or trios. Give each pair a pingpong ball. Demonstrate how to tilt your head back, put the narrow end of the funnel into your mouth, and drop the ball into the funnel.

Say: **When your ball is in the funnel, blow as hard as you can into the narrow end of your funnel. See if you can blow the ball up and out of the funnel.**

Let children take turns with the pingpong balls in their pairs. Kids can cheer each other on as they try to blow the balls up into the air and out of the funnels, but they will not be able to actually accomplish this task. After several minutes, have children put the supplies away and gather for discussion.

Ask: • **Now do you think you're strong? Why or why not?**

• **Why couldn't we blow the pingpong ball out of the funnel?**

• **What are other things we're just not strong enough to do?**

• **What makes you feel strong? What makes you feel weak?**

Say: **God works in surprising and unexpected ways, even with the invisible air around us. Just as the pingpong ball was too much for us to blow away, our problems are often too big to be solved without God's strength. Today we'll be learning that ⬤ we can be strong because our power comes from God. Let's see what the Bible teaches us about this.**

helping the child carry the weight. Demonstrate how to open and close the flaps quickly to create an animated effect. It looks as if Jesus is helping the child lift the problems of his or her life.

Say: **The Bible tells us that we can be strong in the Lord and in his power. God's power is greater than our own. Fill in the box that tells how you need God's power.**

When children have finished, have them place these papers in their Travel Journals.

**HOME AGAIN PRAYER**  (up to 5 minutes)

Say: **Think of what you wrote on your Souvenir page. Silently ask God to give you his strength for this need.**

After a moment of silence, pray: **Almighty God, we ask that you strengthen us to do powerful things in your name. We want to be strong in every way, physically, mentally and spiritually. Only you can make us strong. We are sorry when we try to do things on our own without asking for your help. We know that you are so strong and can do anything; please help us trust you so that we rely on you and grow strong in our faith.**

**SCENIC ROUTE →**  Discuss Bible heroes such as Samson, Moses, and Esther. Talk about how they used God's power to help others.

Ask: • **What Bible hero would you most like to be? Why?**

Ask the children to share ways they could use God's power to help others.

**SCENIC ROUTE →**  Have the kids list stories of God's power in action, such as the parting of the Red Sea, the walls of Jericho falling down, or the defeat of Goliath. Using poster board and markers, have your students create a colorful advertisement to tell others in the church about God's power. Ask them to think of reasons we know that God is all-powerful, and have them put these into their advertisements as words and drawings.

Photocopy this page and cut the problem situations into slips as indicated.
These will be used in the "Super Strength" activity on page *37*.

---

**Jenny is afraid of the dark.**

---

**Jordan broke his leg and has to use crutches for two months.**

---

**Cameron is moving to a new state and will have to go to a new school.**

---

**There is a girl at school spreading mean lies about Amber.**

---

**An older boy punched Drew in the stomach while they were at the bus stop.**

---

**Logan's parents fight a lot. Logan is worried they might get divorced.**

---

**There have been a lot of stories in the news about war and mean people. Jack is afraid.**

---

**Shakira's grandfather has cancer.**

---

**Ian doesn't have any friends.**

---

## Strength From God

"Finally, be strong in the Lord and in his mighty power" (EPHESIANS 6:10).

I need power from God to...

# JOURNEY 5

# The Belt of Truth

**Pathway Point:**  God's true Word helps us do what's right.

**In-Focus Verse:** "Stand firm then, with the belt of truth buckled around your waist" (Ephesians 6:14a).

## Travel Itinerary

What is truth? Our society says that truth is relative, and there is no absolute truth. This viewpoint makes it hard for children (and adults) to know what to believe and what to hold on to.

We need to assure children that there is a reliable source of truth—the Bible. Because God's Word is true, we can depend on it to guide us. And just as a belt holds up an important part of our wardrobe, the belt of truth holds us up spiritually, keeping our armor in place, and it holds our faith together. With this belt wrapped snugly about us, we can make good choices and remain strong in our faith.

Use this lesson to let children know there *is* truth, and that depending on God's Word can lead them into making wise choices.

**DEPARTURE PRAYER** (up to 5 minutes)

Have children gather in a tight circle. Give one child an end of the rope, then walk around the outside of the circle, wrapping the rope around the entire group. Encourage kids to move close together as you wind the rope around, including yourself within the group. When you reach the end of the rope, give the end to a child to hold.

Say: **Let's imagine that this rope is a belt. Today we're going to be learning about a belt mentioned in the Bible. Just like this belt around us, the belt we'll learn about holds things together and keeps an important kind of "clothing" from falling off.**

Pray: **Lord, there are many lies that pull us away from you. As we learn about the belt of truth today, help us remember to draw close to the truth and let the truth of your Word guide our lives. Help us learn that**  **God's true Word helps us do what's right. In Jesus' name, amen.**

Remove the rope and set it aside.

**TOUR GUIDE TIP** The activities in this book have been designed for multi-age groups. Select from the activities, or adapt them as needed for your class.

**Item to Pack:** a long rope

**SCENIC ROUTE →** Provide a belt for each child to wear during this lesson. You can make belts from rope, long lengths of felt, or braided yarn.

**FUN FACT** People use their belts to hold up their pants, but they also hang useful things on them. Phones, tools, keys, and other objects are often seen dangling from belts. What could you hang on your belt?

**1st STOP DISCOVERY** (15 minutes)

## That's the Truth!

Children will see how truth holds firm against lies.

**Items to Pack:** a pair of oversized men's pants with belt loops, an old belt, marker, paper, masking tape
Prepare by writing "God's Word" in bold letters on the belt.

Let several children try on the pants over their clothes. Point out that these pants will not stay up without the help of a belt—they'll just keep falling down!

Have an adult helper put on the pants over his or her clothes (or put them on yourself). Show kids the belt and what you've written on it, then put the belt through the loops on the pants and have the helper secure the belt.

Say: [Name of person wearing pants] **really wants to keep these pants on! But heavy things keep tugging at the pants, trying to pull them off. The things that tug at them are lies. Let's see if God's Word is strong enough to keep these lies from tugging off the pants.**

Have kids call out lies that might hurt them or make them feel afraid. Guide children toward lies that children might believe about themselves or the world around them. These might be silly lies ("There are monsters under your bed") or serious lies ("You're not important").

As children call out various lies, write these on pieces of paper and tape them to the legs of the pants. As children call out their suggestions, suggest and write these lies as well:

- You're not important.
- It's OK to say bad or mean words.
- No one loves you.
- You're all alone in this world.

When the pants are covered with lies, give a few gentle tugs on the legs of the pants. Say: **These lies are heavy, and they sure do weigh down these pants. But so far the belt of truth is holding firm. We're going to come back to these pants in a little while and see exactly why that belt is so strong. But first, let's look into the Bible to find out about some young men who really wrapped the belt of God's truth tightly around themselves. From their example we'll see that  God's true Word helps us do what's right.**

Have the person wearing the pants continue to wear them, and the papers taped to them, during the next section of the lesson.

**TOUR GUIDE TIP** Find an extra-large pair of men's pants and an old belt at a secondhand store. Then, instead of taping papers with words on them onto the pants, you can write directly on the pants with a marker.

**TOUR GUIDE TIP** Prepare your volunteer ahead of time so that he or she is wearing appropriate attire under the oversized pants. Ask this person to ham it up during the activity, making it clear that he or she does not want to lose these pants!

**TOUR GUIDE TIP** Make an overhead transparency of the children wearing armor on page 8. Show this to the children as you talk about the belt of truth, and use a colorful marker to highlight the belts the children in the picture are wearing.

43

**Items to Pack:** white robe or large shirt; yellow, orange, and red crepe paper streamers; a Bible; a hat; bell or other simple musical instrument

**SCENIC ROUTE →** Add extra impact to this account by putting red bulbs into your light fixtures and turning on a space heater to simulate the heat of the furnace (be sure kids don't touch it).

**STORY EXCURSION**

(15 minutes)

## Into the Fire

Children will participate in telling the story of the fiery furnace.

Open your Bible to Daniel 3 and show children that what you're going to share comes from God's Word. Say: **In Daniel 3 is a true story of three young men who were very brave and who loved God so much that they were willing to stand up for God's truth. Their names were Shadrach, Meshach, and Abednego, and I'm going to need everyone to help tell what happened to them.**

Recruit three children to play the young men. Explain that each time you say the names Shadrach, Meshach and Abednego, they should shout, "We will not bow down!" Have another child put on the white robe or shirt and stand off to the side. Ask another child to play the part of King Nebuchadnezzar, and have this child wear the hat. Give all the other children about a foot of either red, orange, or yellow crepe paper. Have children set these aside until they're called for in the script.

Explain that kids should act out the story as you tell it. Be sure to pause occasionally as you read so that kids can act out their parts.

Say: **The king in those days was named Nebuchadnezzar. He was a proud man who thought he was pretty important. He walked around with his chest puffed out. Nebuchadnezzar thought he was so important that he decided to have a statue made of himself. It was ninety feet high, nine feet wide, and it was made of gold.**

Compare this to a building or structure in your community that would be equal to this in height so that children can get an idea of the size of the statue.

Say: **Then Nebuchadnezzar gathered everyone to come see this image. Everyone, gather closely around Nebuchadnezzar. Shadrach, Meshach and Abednego were among those invited, so they should join in with everyone else.**

**When everyone was there, an announcement was made. When the music started, everyone was to bow down to the statue and worship it. Nebuchadnezzar wanted everyone to worship him as if he were God! And if anyone refused, they would be thrown into a fiery furnace and burned to death. He was serious about this!**

**So the music sounded.** (Ring the bell or sound the other instrument.) **Everyone bowed down to the statue—everyone except Shadrach,**

44

Meshach, and Abednego, that is. These young men just stood there. They knew the truth of God's Word that told them only to worship God. So they refused to bow down.

King Nebuchadnezzar had the three young men come stand before him. He shook his fist at them and told them they had to bow down and worship. He was going to give them one more chance, and this time they'd better obey or it was off to the fire!

Pause the story for a moment and ask the kids what they would do if they were in the shoes of Shadrach, Meshach, and Abednego. Ask them to think honestly about their decision. Then continue with the story.

Say: **Shadrach, Meshach, and Abednego shook their heads at the king. They said they didn't need another chance. They were not going to bow down. They said, "If we are thrown into the blazing furnace, the God we serve is able to save us from it, and he will rescue us from your hand, O king. But even if he does not, we want you to know, O king, that we will not serve your gods or worship the image of gold you have set up." Shadrach, Meshach, and Abednego knew that God had the power to save them, and even if God chose not to save them, they were still going to obey God and not worship anyone else.**

**This made the king furious! He was jumping up and down and shaking his fists, he was so mad. He ordered the furnace to be made seven times hotter!**

Have all the kids with streamers begin gently waving them as if they are the flames of the fire.

Say: **The strongest soldiers tied up Shadrach, Meshach, and Abednego and threw them into the blazing fire. It was so hot that the flames actually killed the soldiers that threw the three young men into the furnace! The king looked into the fire, expecting to see Shadrach, Meshach, and Abednego dead in the flames, but instead he saw them walking around in the furnace, and there was a fourth man with them—a man who the king believed was an angel!** (Have the child in white join the others in the "furnace.")

**The king called Shadrach, Meshach, and Abednego out of the furnace.** Have the children set their "flames" aside. **He looked at their clothes. They weren't burnt! He sniffed at their hair. It didn't even smell like smoke! King Nebuchadnezzar began to praise the true God, and he even gave Shadrach, Meshach, and Abednego a promotion!**

Have everyone return their props and sit down. Ask:

• **Why wouldn't Shadrach, Meshach, and Abednego bow down and worship the statue? What Bible truth does that go against?**

• **Why do you think Shadrach, Meshach, and Abednego were brave enough to stand up for the truth?**

• **How did knowing  God's true Word help them do what was right?**

• **Who do you think was the fourth person that appeared in the furnace with them?**

• **What is a truth that you need to stand up for?**

• **What makes it hard to stand up for the truth?**

Say: **Shadrach, Meshach, and Abednego were wearing the belt of truth. This isn't a literal belt like you use to hold up your pants. Instead, it's like a picture that helps us understand how important truth is in our lives—and how knowing the truth and believing  God's true Word helps us do what's right. Let's get back to that pair of pants being dragged down by all those lies, to see how God's true Word gets rid of the lies.**

SCENIC ROUTE

Memorizing God's Word can tighten the belt of truth around your waist. During class, each time you say, "Tighten your belt," have kids freeze in place and say a verse about truth, such as 1 Corinthians 13:6, which says, "Love does not delight in evil but rejoices with the truth."

**Items to Pack:** person wearing pants from earlier activity, Bibles

ADVENTURES IN GROWING

(15 minutes)
## Belted in Truth

Kids will use Bible verses to demonstrate that truth holds up against lies.

Have the person wearing the oversized pants return to the front of the room. Say: **I know a few verses in the Bible that might show us the truth about some of these lies.**

Have children form four groups. Assign each group one of the following verses to look up and read.

• Matthew 28:20b

• John 3:16

• Ephesians 4:29

• Luke 12:7

Say: **Read your verse and decide how it proves that one or more of the things written on these pants are lies.**

Allow time for children to read their verses and discuss what they read. Have the person wearing the pants move from group to group so the kids can look more closely at the lies and determine how their verse stands up against one or more of them.

After a few minutes, have someone from each group read their verse aloud and share their findings. Then take the lie that has been discussed off the pants. If you have written the lies directly on the pants, draw a line though that lie.

Say: **The Bible is full of truth. There is nothing in the Bible that's a lie, because it is God's Word. When we start being dragged down by lies and they lead us into bad choices, we can turn to God's Word, the Bible, to show us the truth.** Ask:

• **How did knowing the truth help Shadrach, Meshach, and Abednego make good choices?**

• **How does knowing the truth about these lies help you make good choices?**

• **How can believing lies lead us into making bad choices?**

Say: **A belt holds up an important part of our clothing. The belt of truth holds us up when we're being attacked with lies. Ephesians 6:14 tells us to "Stand firm then, with the belt of truth buckled around your waist." This means that when we know and obey God's true Word, it helps us do what's right.**

## SOUVENIRS → (10 minutes)
## Protected by Truth

Children will do an art project that reminds them of the Bible story.

**Items to Pack:** copies of the "Belt of Truth" handout (p. 49); crayons (including white crayons); red, yellow, and orange watercolor paints; paintbrushes

Give each child a "Belt of Truth" handout. Read the verses aloud together and ask kids to think of situations where these verses might help them make good choices.

Let children color the pictures of Shadrach, Meshach, and Abednego. Let them take turns using white crayons to draw a fourth figure beside the young men. Then have children brush over their coloring with the orange, red, and yellow watercolor paints. Explain that they should make the young men look as if they're in the fiery furnace. Kids will notice that when they apply the paint, the crayon will resist the water and will allow the figure drawn in white crayon to appear.

After the pictures dry, have children add them to their Travel Journals.

**Item to Pack:** rope used in earlier activity

**HOME AGAIN PRAYER** (5 minutes)

Have children again stand in a circle, and wrap the rope around them as a giant belt.

Say: **We've learned today that** 🌀 **God's true Word helps us do what's right. And when we wear the belt of truth, we can stand stronger and not be distracted by lies.**

Pray: **Lord, as we are wrapped together with this belt, help us to remember the belt of truth and the power that truth has to help us make good choices. Thank you that your words to us are always true. In Jesus' name, amen.**

# Belt of Truth

## "Stand firm then, with the *belt of truth* buckled around your waist" (EPHESIANS 6:14a).

"Love does not delight in evil but rejoices with the truth" (1 Corinthians 13:6).

"Every word of God is flawless; he is a shield to those who take refuge in him" (Proverbs 30:5).

"Then you will know the truth, and the truth will set you free" (John 8:32).

"Finally, brothers, whatever is true, whatever is noble, whatever is right, whatever is pure, whatever is lovely, whatever is admirable—if anything is excellent or praiseworthy—think about such things" (Philippians 4:8).

# The Breastplate of Righteousness

**Pathway Point:** 🌐 We can trust God to protect our hearts.

**In-Focus Verse:** "Stand firm then...with the breastplate of righteousness in place" (Ephesians 6:14).

## Travel Itinerary

A child's heart is tender. Seemingly small injuries can wound a child's sense of personal value and lovability. Failing at a new task. Disappointment on a parent's face. Harsh words from a friend. Why do such wounds sometimes leave scars? Surely the answer lies partly in the nature of spiritual warfare. Satan will use any opportunity to cause us to question God's love and our worth in his eyes. Satan wants to crush our hearts and kill our faith.

But our mighty God will not permit Satan to destroy his children. God protects tender hearts with the breastplate of righteousness. The Bible tells us we do not deserve and cannot earn righteousness, a right standing with God. Yet through faith in Jesus, God declares we are right with him. Use this lesson to help children understand that God's armor holds fast against the messages of Satan. We are loved...we are accepted...because we are God's.

**DEPARTURE PRAYER** (up to 5 minutes)

Before class, cut one 5x6-inch heart from the red construction paper.

Have kids sit in a circle. Say: **Put your hand over your heart. God created our physical hearts to pump blood and keep us alive and healthy. Our physical hearts remind us how wise and wonderful God is in creating our bodies. Today, however, we'll be talking about a different kind of heart. For example, sometimes we say a person has a heart for God or someone has a broken heart. What do you think that means?** Listen to responses. **When we talk about our heart in that way, we mean the part of us that makes us unique, different from anyone else. Our personality, feelings, thoughts, and hopes make each one of us the special person we are.**

Ask: • What might people say that would hurt your heart?

**• Have you ever felt that someone didn't like you? What did you do then?**

---

**TOUR GUIDE TIP**

The activities in this book have been designed for multi-age groups. Select from the activities, or adapt them as needed for your class.

**Items to Pack:** red construction paper, scissors

**FUN FACT**

Our physical hearts give amazing testimony to the creative power of God. Five to seven weeks after conception, an unborn baby's developing heart begins beating. Over an average life span, the human heart will beat more than 2.5 billion times!

• **How do you think God feels toward us when we feel sad or hurt?**

Say: **Our hearts are very special to God because he loves each one of us. He doesn't want our hearts to feel hurt or torn. ◐ We can trust God to protect our hearts.**

As you pray, pass the heart around the circle. Tell kids to tear off a small piece of the heart before passing it on to the next child.

Pray: **Dear God, thank you for making us one-of-a-kind and treasuring our hearts. Sometimes things happen that make our hearts feel sad or hurt or torn. People say or do things that make us feel unloved. Our enemy, Satan, wants us to doubt your love for us. Help us trust you to protect our hearts and remember you always love us, no matter what. Amen.**

### 1ˢᵗ STOP DISCOVERY (10 minutes)
### Heart Hits

Kids will experience our need for protection from hurtful words and actions in this active game.

Before class, make two poster-board breastplates with the words "I trust in Jesus!" written on them. Breastplates should be simple rectangles with rounded corners, approximately 18 inches tall and 12 inches wide. Use a hole punch to create holes where indicated, and tie 18-inch pieces of yarn as indicated.

Open your Bible to Ephesians 6:14 and show kids that what you're reading comes from God's Word.

Say: **We've been learning that God is most powerful and that we don't have to be afraid. He's given us armor to protect us from enemies that try to hurt our faith. Today we're going to learn that ◐ we can trust God to protect our hearts. Ephesians 6:14 says, "Stand firm then...with the breastplate of righteousness in place." A breastplate is a piece of armor that covers the entire front of the chest. It protects the heart, lungs and abdominal organs. Righteousness means being right with God. Things are OK between God and us because he promises to forgive and accept those who believe in Jesus.**

Ask: • **What are some things people say that can hurt our feelings?**

• **What are some things people do that might make us feel unloved?**

Say: **We're going to play a game to see how it feels to be the target of hurtful words and actions.** Distribute markers and one cardboard tube to

**TOUR GUIDE TIP**

Make an overhead transparency of the children wearing armor on page 8. Show this to the children as you talk about the breastplate of righteousness, and use a colorful marker to highlight the breastplates that the children in the picture are wearing.

**Items to Pack:** Bible, poster board, markers, yarn, hole punch, two large paper hearts (approximately 15 inches tall and 10 inches wide), masking tape, paper towel tubes or gift wrap tubes cut into 12-inch sections

I trust in Jesus!

51

**SCENIC ROUTE →** Involve kids in making the breastplates. Have pictures available of various types of armor to stimulate kids' thinking. Provide markers, yarn, foil, glue and glitter for kids to use in creating breastplates that show God is most powerful. Have them include the words "I trust in Jesus!"

**TOUR GUIDE TIP** Be sure the volunteers you choose are confident and will not take the actions of this game personally. Or have adult or teen volunteers take these roles.

**TOUR GUIDE TIP** Help kids play safely in this energetic activity. Don't allow kids to hit or stab at each other with the tubes. Tell them that simply touching the heart counts.

each child. **On your tube, write words or draw a picture of something that could make someone feel hurt or unloved.** Give children time to work.

Choose two volunteers and tape a large heart on each volunteer's chest. Have the volunteers stand back-to-back. Gather the remaining children in a circle around them.

Say: **When people say or do mean things to us, it can feel like being wounded in the heart. These tubes are like hurtful swords. When I give the signal, use your sword to try to touch the heart taped to one of our volunteers. If you touch any part of the heart, you've wounded that person. Volunteers, you can use your hands to protect your heart, but you can't run away.**

Signal children to begin and allow them to play for one minute. Then have children put down their tubes.

Ask: • **How did it feel to get attacked by those swords?**

• **How do you feel when someone says or does something mean to you?**

• **How did you feel when you saw our volunteers get attacked by so many swords?**

• **How do you feel after you say or do something that hurts someone else?**

Next, tie the poster-board breastplates on the volunteers so that their paper hearts are covered. Have children read the message on the breastplates aloud. Play the game again for one minute, then have children put all the supplies away.

Ask: • **What was the same or different about using the breastplates?**

• **What happened when the swords tried to touch the hearts this time?**

• **If these were really hurtful things instead of cardboard tubes, how would the breastplate have helped our volunteers?**

Say: **Sometimes things happen that cause us to feel hurt, sad, or like we're not any good. Our enemy, Satan, tries to use those feelings to make us doubt God's love. But God is most powerful and he designed spiritual armor to protect us. God gives us the breastplate of righteousness to protect our hearts. When we believe in Jesus we can know we are right with God. He *does* love us. We *are* special to him and ◗ we can trust God to protect our hearts. Let's look into the Bible to learn more about this.**

(15 minutes)
## God's Promise

Children will make background scenes and participate in telling the Bible story.

**Items to Pack:** Bible, black construction paper, sharpened pencils, newspaper (optional), flashlights (one for every two children)

Have kids form pairs, and give each pair a piece of black construction paper, two sharpened pencils, and a flashlight. Show kids how to lay the black paper on the carpeting or newspaper and use the pencils to poke tiny holes in the paper. Allow a few minutes for each pair to make an arrangement of these "star" holes.

Turn off the lights in the room, and let kids take turns holding their pictures and shining the flashlight on the back. The tiny points of light they've created will look like stars on the ceiling.

Turn off the flashlights and have pairs sit together in a circle on the floor. Keep room lights dim while telling the story. Tell kids to be ready to display their star pictures at the appropriate part of the story. Open your Bible to Genesis 15.

Say: **Today's story comes from the book of Genesis and is about a couple name Abram and Sarai. They felt sad because they had never had any children. Now they were too old to expect to have a baby anymore. God loved Abram and wanted to bless him. God spoke to Abram one night. "Don't be afraid, Abram. I will protect you and bring good things into your life."**

**Abram answered God, "Nothing will seem good because I don't have a child to share it with."**

**Then God made Abram a promise. "You are going to have a son." God took Abram outside and told him to look up at the stars.** Have one member of each pair shine the light behind the paper while the other lies on the floor and looks at the stars.

**God told him, "See if you can count all the stars in the sky. Your son will grow up to have children, and his children will have children, and their children will have children. Your many descendants will be like the many stars in the sky!"**

Have kids try to count the stars they can see. Then have children exchange places with their partners to let them see and count stars.

Ask: • **How many stars do you think are on all our star papers?**

• **How many stars do you think Abram saw?**

• **Have you counted stars at night? How many stars do you think God created?**

**SCENIC
ROUTE
→** Set up an in-home star projector before kids arrive. These use a light source to illumine a variety of constellations on the ceiling of a dark room. Turn it on as children are arriving and again during the Story Excursion.

**TOUR
GUIDE
TIP** This project works best on a carpeted floor. If your classroom has hard flooring, provide children with small stacks of newspaper on which they can place their construction paper to poke holes.

**FUN
FACT** How many stars are visible from your home at night? If you live where city lights obscure the fainter stars, you may see about 300 stars. If you live in the country where skies are darker, you may see what Abram probably saw—up to 3500 stars! Our own Milky Way galaxy contains more than 100 billion stars, and there are thought to be billions of galaxies in the universe, each one home to millions or billions of stars.

**SCENIC ROUTE →**

*Star Snacks*—Use star-shaped cookie cutters to cut shapes from slices of bread. Have kids spread their stars with butter or margarine, then sprinkle them with colored sugar.

Say: **Even after God's promise, Abram and Sarai waited many years for their baby. It seemed impossible that such old people would have a baby after waiting so long. But instead of worrying that God didn't love him or might not keep his promise—Abram believed. His trust in God was like a breastplate keeping his heart and faith from being crushed by disappointment. Abram believed God could do anything, even things that seemed impossible. His faith got stronger. God protected his heart.**

**Of course God *did* keep his promise. Abram had a son named Isaac. Isaac had children, and Isaac's children had children—a huge family. In fact, many years later, one of Abram's descendants was Jesus, the Savior God promised to save people from their sins.**

Ask: **• How did trusting God protect Abram's heart?**

**• What do you trust God to do for you?**

Say: **Just as God loved and blessed Abram, God loves and blesses us. We can trust God like Abram did. We don't have to worry that God doesn't love us or won't keep his promises. We *know* he loves us and will *always* keep his promises. Just as God protected Abram's heart, ◐ we can trust God to protect our hearts.**

**Items to Pack:** Bibles, newsprint, markers

**ADVENTURES IN GROWING**

**(10 minutes)**

## Trusting God to Make Us Right

Kids will look into God's Word to discover how to be right with God.

Say: **The Bible tells us God is perfect and never sins. God doesn't like sin because it hurts the people he loves. But all of us *do* sin. Sin separates us from God and makes us *not right* with him. No matter how hard we try to be good, we still do things God doesn't like. But God loves us so much that he sent Jesus to save us. Jesus died on the cross and took the punishment for our sin. When we trust in Jesus, God forgives all the *not-right* things we do and say. God says we are *right* with him. Being righteous means things are OK between God and us. He forgives and accepts us because we trust in Jesus.**

Have children form three groups. Give each group a Bible, newsprint, and markers. Include both older and younger children in each group. Within each group, have kids choose a Leader, a Reader, a Writer, and a Reporter. If you have smaller groups, children may choose more than one role. Leaders will guide the

**TOUR GUIDE TIP**

Abram and Abraham are different names for the same man. God changed Abram's name as part of his covenant promise (Genesis 17:5). *Abram* means "exalted father." *Abraham* means "father of many."

discussion and make sure everyone has a chance to contribute. Readers will find and read the verses. Writers will write or draw what their group discusses, and the Reporters will convey their group's findings to the class.

Assign groups the following verses to research:

Group 1: Romans 4:18-19

Group 2: Romans 4:20-22

Group 3: Romans 4:23-25

If your class has more than twenty children, form groups of five or six and assign the verses to more than one group. Write the following questions on the board or on newsprint so groups can refer to them independently.

Ask: • **What did Abraham do to be right with God?**

• **How can we be right with God?**

• **What has God promised that we can trust him to do?**

While children work, walk between groups and answer any questions. After allowing a few minutes for reading and discussion, gather the class and invite Reporters to share what their groups discovered.

Say: **We can trust God's promise to save us when we have a relationship with Jesus. We could never be right with God by not sinning —that would be impossible for us. The only way for people to be right with God is to trust in Jesus.**  **We can trust God to protect our hearts with the breastplate of righteousness. When we sin, or feel hurt or worried, Satan wants us to doubt God's love and promises. But we can know we are right with God—loved, forgiven and accepted by him—when we trust in Jesus.**

**FUN FACT** Kids today rarely see armor, but the people of Paul's time would have been very familiar with it. Cities were guarded by Roman soldiers who wore breastplates made of strips of metal held together with leather straps and bronze fittings.

## SOUVENIRS → (10 minutes)
## Heart Armor

This craft demonstrates how God's armor protects our hearts.

**Items to Pack:** card stock, scissors, aluminum foil, unsharpened pencils, small bowls of water

Before class, cut two hearts per child from card stock. Make hearts approximately 6 inches wide by 5 inches tall. Cut aluminum foil into 7-inch squares. On tables, set out one small bowl of water for every five children. Gather children to sit on the floor.

Say: **God wants to protect our hearts. He wants us to remember that even when we have troubles or make mistakes, or when others say hurtful things, God still loves us. Just like Abram, we can trust God to protect out hearts with the breastplate of righteousness. When we trust in Jesus, we know we are right with God.**

Distribute two hearts and one square of foil to each child.

Say: **Let's do an activity to see how God's armor protects our hearts. Leave one heart where you are sitting and bring the other to one of the bowls of water. Use your fingers to sprinkle a few drops onto the heart.** Allow children time to work.

Ask: • **What happened to the hearts?**

• **How is this like when we feel hurt or no good?**

Say: **These hearts were unprotected and they were hurt by the water. Satan also wants to hurt our hearts and make us doubt God's love. Now let's make armor like a breastplate to protect the second heart.**

Show kids how to lay the heart on top of the foil and gently fold the foil around the edges of the heart, covering one side completely. Turn the heart over so the foil side is up. Have kids use unsharpened pencils to write "I trust Jesus" into the foil. Remind kids to press lightly to avoid tearing the foil. Have kids return to the bowl and sprinkle drops of water onto their foil-covered hearts.

Ask: • **What happened to the hearts this time?**

• **What do you think the heart looks like underneath the armor?**

• **How is this like the way God's armor protects our hearts?**

Say: **God keeps our hearts safe with the breastplate of righteousness. No matter what happens in our life or how we feel, we remember that trusting in Jesus makes us right with God. Satan can't hurt us because God is most powerful. He loves us and he is on our side.**

Have kids keep the armored heart for use in the Home Again Prayer.

**TOUR GUIDE TIP** If children seem hesitant to pray aloud, help increase their comfort level by giving examples of one-sentence prayers. Remind them that they can talk to God the way they would talk to a friend. Encourage kids to grow in prayer, but do not force anyone to pray aloud.

**HOME AGAIN PRAYER** (up to 5 minutes)

Gather kids to stand shoulder-to-shoulder in a circle with their backs toward the center. Tell kids to hold their Heart Armor project over their hearts.

Say: **God protects our hearts one by one, but when we gather together as God's people, he also protects us as a group, the church.**

**Let's close with a circle prayer. Each of us will pray one sentence telling God how we feel about trusting Jesus. You might thank God for sending Jesus to make us right with him. Or you might ask God for a strong faith like Abram's. Hold your Heart Armor over your own heart to help you remember our verse, "Stand firm...with the breastplate of righteousness in place" (Ephesians 6:14).**

Allow each child to pray. Conclude with a one-sentence prayer asking God to use his armor to protect these children in the coming week.

Have kids place their armored hearts in a pocket in their Travel Journals or glue them to the front as a reminder of God's love in protecting his children.

# Fitted Feet

**Pathway Point:**  We can be ready to tell others about God's peace.

**In-Focus Verse:** "And with your feet fitted with the readiness that comes from the gospel of peace" (Ephesians 6:15).

## Travel Itinerary

Have you ever put on a pair of new shoes and felt that you could run faster and jump higher? Shoes make a difference! A football player would never run onto the playing field wearing sandals, and a basketball player would never jog down the court wearing cleats. Instead, athletes wear shoes that support them and make them ready to play the game ahead.

The footwear provided as part of God's armor make us ready as well—ready to share the good news of Jesus Christ with others. When we're ready and motivated, we can have peace in our hearts as well as true peace to pass on. Use this journey to help children spring into action and spread God's peace and love.

**DEPARTURE PRAYER** (up to 5 minutes)

Say: **We've been learning about the armor of God, and today we're going to learn about the footwear that goes with this armor. So let's use our feet as we pray.**

Have children form small groups of five or six and huddle in their groups. Have the tallest person in each group begin by completing this sentence prayer: "Lord, help me be ready to ____." They might finish the sentence with words like *listen, be kind, help others*, and so on. When the first child is finished praying, this child should use his or her foot to tap the foot of the child on the right. This is continued until each child has prayed.

**1st STOP DISCOVERY** (15 minutes)
## Ready to Run

Children will consider footwear that helps people be ready for different jobs.

Have children form groups of three or four, and give each group a pair of shoes. Say: **Decide who would wear your pair of shoes, and how these shoes would help that person.**

Give groups a few minutes to discuss, then have each group choose one person to put on the shoes, stand, and tell who he or she is and how the shoes help. For example, a child wearing snow boots could say, "I'm a girl getting ready to play in the snow, and these boots will protect my feet from the cold," or a child wearing cleats could say, "I'm a football player and these shoes will help my feet grip the ground so I can run faster."

Allow each group to make their presentation, then ask:

• **What would happen to your person if he or she couldn't wear these shoes?**

• **If you don't have your shoes on, are you ready for school? for playing a sport? for hiking over rocky ground? Why or why not?**

• **If you were going hiking over sharp rocks and discovered you'd forgotten your shoes, would you feel worried or feel peaceful? Why?**

Say: **Shoes help us to be ready for different activities. They protect our feet from rain and snow, and from hot pavement or sharp objects. Special shoes give us support for specific tasks like running, fishing, swimming, or climbing rocks. God also has special shoes for us to wear. Ephesians 6:15 tells us to have our "feet fitted with the readiness that comes from the gospel of peace." These shoes help us be ready to share God's love and peace. We're going to check out an account from the Bible to help us understand that ◗ we can be ready to tell others about God's peace.**

## (15 Minutes)
## Rough but Ready

Kids will explore the account of Paul and Silas in prison, and consider how they were ready to share the gospel at all times.

Prepare ahead of time by taping lengths of black crepe paper around the edges of a table to create a jail cell. If you have a large number of children, you can create more than one jail cell by using several tables.

Show children your Bible and say: **The Bible tells us in Acts 16 about two men who were always ready to tell others about God and the peace that comes from knowing God. Let's retell their story.**

Choose children to play the roles of Paul, Silas, and the jailer. Have the remaining children form two groups. One will be the crowd, and the other group will be prisoners. Explain that as you tell the story you'll indicate actions for the kids to do. Be sure to pause at the appropriate times for kids to act their roles. To begin, have everyone sit on the floor.

For sanitary reasons, have children wear their socks when putting on the shoes.

**Items to Pack:** table, tape, black crepe paper, Bible

**SCENIC ROUTE →** Make this story really come alive by building a jail cell. Stuff large paper grocery bags with crumpled newspaper to make bricks, and stack them to make walls. Place toy bugs and rats on the floor, drape chains and padlocks over a bench, and recruit burly volunteers to be the guards.

Say: **Once there were two men named Paul and Silas. Let's meet them now.**

Have Paul and Silas stand and wave.

Say: **Paul and Silas loved God very much, and traveled around telling people about God. They were always ready to tell about God's love and the peace that comes from knowing God. Let's watch as Paul and Silas walk around our group, smiling, shaking hands, and saying, "God loves you!"**

Allow a moment for Paul and Silas to do this, then say: **Not everyone was happy about the words and actions of Paul and Silas. One day, they healed a girl who was a slave. Her owners were not happy about this. So they grabbed Paul and Silas and brought them to the rulers. A crowd gathered.**

Have the crowd gather closely around Paul and Silas.

Say: **The crowd murmured with anger. They shook their fists. They accused Paul and Silas of trying to cause trouble. So the rulers said that Paul and Silas should be severely beaten—and that's what happened. But we won't act out the part where they get beaten. And then they were thrown into jail.**

Have Paul and Silas get under the table and into the jail cell you've created. Have the other prisoners join them.

Say: **The jailer was ordered to guard Paul and Silas carefully, so he put them in an inner cell and locked their feet up in stocks. Then he lay down to sleep.**

**You would think that Paul and Silas would be angry, or afraid, or crying in pain. But instead, they did something very surprising. They started to sing and pray! The other prisoners listened to them. Let's listen too!**

Have Paul and Silas hum or sing for a moment.

Say: **Suddenly there was a violent earthquake! Everything started shaking and rumbling and rolling! The doors of the jail flew open and all the chains came loose. The jailer woke up. He thought all the prisoners had escaped, so he drew his sword to kill himself. But Paul shouted, "Don't harm yourself! We're all here!"**

**The jailer rushed over to Paul and Silas, fell before them, and asked, "What must I do to be saved?" Paul and Silas were ready to tell him exactly what he wanted to know. They told him, "Believe in the**

Lord Jesus, and you will be saved." And that's just what happened!

Have all your actors return to their seats, then ask:

• **Why do you think Paul and Silas were able to have such peace and joy even when they were beaten and in prison?**

• **What were they ready to tell the jailer and anyone else?**

• **How do you think they got to the point where they were always ready to tell others about God?**

• **How did peace come into the jailer's life because Paul and Silas were ready?**

Say: **Paul and Silas had on those shoes of readiness. They were excited and motivated to tell the jailer about God's peace and love. Let's do an activity that will help us think of ways we can be ready too.**

**Items to Pack:** white paper, masking tape, markers

**ADVENTURES IN GROWING**

(15 minutes)
## Hop to It!

Children will consider ways they can be ready to share God's love and peace with others.

Give each child a sheet of paper and a marker. Say: **Let's make a giant hopscotch game across our room. Each person will make one square for our game. Think of something that keeps you from feeling ready to tell others about God's peace. It might be that you're afraid of what people will say, or that you're not sure what to say, or something else. Or there may be something that's keeping you from having peace in your life. Write a few words about what keeps you from being ready to share God's peace and love, or words that tell what keeps you from having peace.**

As children finish their papers, have them bring them to you. Begin taping them to the floor to make one large hopscotch pattern across your room.

When the hopscotch area is completed, have children form pairs and have each child take off one shoe. Have pairs stand at the beginning of the game, and

**TOUR GUIDE TIP**

Making the hopscotch pattern will go more quickly if you have one or two adult volunteers help you tape the papers to the floor.

let one of the children in the pair toss a shoe randomly onto a square. Let the child hop to that square while the partner walks beside him or her. The child who hopped should pick up the shoe and read to the partner what is written on that square. Ask the partner to think of one solution to the problem written there and to share this with the child standing on the square. For example, if the square says, "I'm afraid my friend will think I'm weird if I invite her to church," the partner might respond, "You could pray and ask God to help you not be afraid." Then have the pair return to the end of the line, and the next time they're at the starting point have the children switch roles.

Play until each child has had a turn at each role, then have children put on their shoes and return to their seats.

Say: **You all came up with good ideas of how  we can be ready to tell others about God's peace and how we can have more peace in our lives. When we have peace in our own lives, it's easier to share that peace with others. And we've learned ways we need to be more ready. Let's make a page for our Travel Journals to show what we've learned today.**

Items to Pack: copies of the "On Your Mark!" handout (p. 64), Bibles, markers or crayons, pencils

**SOUVENIRS** → (10 minutes)
## On Your Mark!

As children complete this page, they'll discover encouraging words from the Bible to help them.

Give each child a copy of the handout. Ask:

• **Have you ever put on a new pair of shoes and felt like you could run faster and jump higher?**

Say: **This is the feeling we can have when our feet are fitted with the readiness that comes from the gospel of peace. We want to be motivated and excited to tell others about God's peace and love. And when our feet are protected with God's armor, Satan is crushed under our feet!**

Have children form pairs and look up the verses on the handout. Pair older children with younger ones. Tell children that they should choose the verse they like the most and write it on the large shoe. Then let kids color the shoes in the picture. When children are finished, have them put these pages into their Travel Journals.

# The Shield of Faith

**Pathway Point:**  Faith acts as a shield against evil.

**In-Focus Verse:** "In addition to all this, take up the shield of faith, with which you can extinguish all the flaming arrows of the evil one" (Ephesians 6:16).

## Travel Itinerary

It's a fact of life that our faith will be tested. There *will* be battles with the enemy. And the battlefield can just as easily be a child's playground, school bus, or cafeteria as it can be any adult forum. The Bible not only acknowledges that we will face battles, but it also provides us with the tools we need in order to win.

One of those tools is the shield of faith. Faith helps us hold up under pressure. It helps us recall times when God has helped us in the past, and gives us assurance that he will be there for us in the future. Faith can bring to mind Bible passages that will encourage and renew our hearts and minds. Faith can ultimately block the arrows Satan throws at us. By remaining firm in our faith we can thwart Satan and emerge victorious. Use this lesson to instill in kids the confidence that *their* faith can hold firm—that they, too, can be victorious in battle.

**TOUR GUIDE TIP** The activities in this book have been designed for multi-age groups. Select from the activities, or adapt them as needed for your class.

**DEPARTURE PRAYER** (up to 5 minutes)

Before class, set up a simple barrier in the center of your meeting area. Place two chairs next to each other and tape a sheet of newsprint between them. On the newsprint write the word *faith* in large letters.

Gather kids on one side of the barrier you created.

Say: **Let's start our time together with a prayer. Today we're going to be talking about needing a shield of faith to protect us from Satan. Think for a moment about what kinds of problems Satan throws at people. Maybe you'll think of anger, fighting, or temptations like cheating or swearing. Those are all hard things to face. But faith in Jesus can shield us from anything Satan has to offer.**

Explain that after you start the prayer, kids will each name one problem Satan might throw at them. Then they'll move behind the newsprint shield where you'll close the prayer.

**Items to Pack:** newsprint, chairs, marker, tape

Pray: **Dear Lord, thank you for giving us faith to use in our fight against Satan. Please help each person have faith enough to fight against these problems.** Have kids each name a problem and move behind the shield. **Thank you, Lord, for helping and protecting us. Help our faith in you grow stronger and stronger.**

**1st STOP DISCOVERY** (15 minutes)
## Where's My Shield?

Use this activity to give kids a concrete illustration of what it's like to face Satan's attacks without a way to defend themselves.

Say: **As we saw in our opening prayer, a shield can be a safe place to hide behind. The Bible says in Ephesians 6:16 that our faith can be a shield to protect us from the flaming arrows that Satan throws at us. Let's see what it's like to have protection from flaming arrows—and what it's like *not* to have protection. First we need some arrows!**

Set out a supply of scrap paper, fabric squares, scissors, and red and yellow curling ribbon. Challenge kids to make paper arrows to use in a game. Rather than make pointed arrows, though, show kids how to wad the scrap paper into a ball and cover it with a fabric square. Tie several lengths of ribbon around the fabric at the top of the paper wad so it looks like a badminton game piece. Curl the ribbon and you've got flaming arrows!

Place a masking tape line across the center of the floor. After kids have made a supply of arrows, have kids form two groups facing each other across the line. Give all of the arrows to one group only. Explain that at your signal, this group will begin throwing the arrows at members of the other group. Kids in the second group will complain that they have no weapons, but continue play anyway. After a minute or so, call time and have groups switch roles. Play again.

Then have kids answer the following questions in their groups. After each question, invite groups to share their answers with the rest of the class.

Ask: • **What was it like having the arrows thrown at you?**

• **How did you feel without any way to protect yourself?**

• **How is that like how it feels sometimes in real life when tough problems come your way?**

• **What would have made you feel safer during this game?**

• **What helps you face problems in real life?**

Say: **When the arrows were being thrown at you in this game, you had no defense. You had no way to protect yourself. That's what it's**

**TOUR GUIDE TIP** Caution kids to make sure that the arrows they make don't have sharp points or edges that could cause eye injury.

like in life when Satan throws problems at someone without faith. The person has no way to fight back. He or she might feel defeated and hopeless.

But that's not the case for someone who has faith! The Bible says that ◐ faith acts as a shield against evil. With faith, we can defend ourselves. We can trust in God. We can face any problem because we know that God is on our side. Even when things get rough and our faith is tested, we can hold on to the knowledge that God loves us and we're never alone.

That makes me think of a guy in the Bible who really had to hold on to his faith during some very tough times. Let's look at this story right now.

**STORY EXCURSION**

(20 minutes)
## A Serious Story

The story of Job's trials—and triumph—will serve as an example to kids the next time they face problems.

Have kids form five groups and give each group a Bible. Have kids read Job 1:1-12 in their groups.

Ask: • **What kind of man was Job?**

• **What did Satan say about Job?**

• **What do you think Satan had planned for Job?**

Say: **Satan had plans for Job, and they weren't going to be happy surprises. They were going to be the flaming arrows that we talked about earlier. Let's find out what those arrows were.**

Explain that each group will read a section of the Bible story, then illustrate it on a poster. After groups have finished drawing, each group will present its poster to the rest of the class. After all of the posters have been hung on the wall in order, your class will have a visual display of Job's trials.

The first group should read Job 1:13-15; the second group, Job 1:16; the third group, Job 1:17; the fourth group, Job 1:18-19; and the fifth group, Job 2:1-8. As kids are reading, give each group a sheet of poster board, crayons, markers, and pens. Have kids work together in their groups to create a poster depicting the events in the section they just read. Remind kids that they'll be presenting the poster to other groups who haven't read that part of the story.

After about ten minutes, tell kids to finish their drawings. Then let groups present their posters in chronological order to the rest of the class, explaining the

**TOUR GUIDE TIP** Make an overhead transparency of the children wearing armor on page 8. Show this to the children as you talk about the shield of faith, and use a colorful marker to highlight the shields that the children in the picture are holding.

**FUN FACT** Some armies have used shields that can link or lock together to form a larger protective wall around them all.

**Items to Pack:** Bibles, poster board, crayons, markers, pens, tape

**FUN FACT** Many Bible scholars believe that Job lived around the same time as Abraham, Isaac, and Jacob.

SCENIC
ROUTE
→

If you have time, let kids work together on a poster that depicts the happy ending to Job's life. Leave the series of posters hanging in your room to remind kids that God is in control and will never desert them.

FUN
FACT

When does a coat communicate? When it's a coat of arms! Knights painted distinctive images on their shields as a means of identification because wearing their full armor concealed their identity.

events that happened to Job. Hang the posters on the wall in order.

Say: **Wow! Those are some flaming arrows from Satan, aren't they?**

Ask: • **How would you have felt if those things had happened to you?**

• **What do you think Job was feeling and thinking?**

• **After all those bad things happened, how do you think Job felt about God? How would you have felt?**

Say: **It's hard to imagine that Job kept his faith in God through all those awful things, but he did! In fact, look at what he said after he had lost his possessions and servants and kids.** Choose a volunteer to read aloud Job 1:20-22. **Later, even after Satan afflicted Job with sores all over his body, Job's faith held firm. Listen to what he said then.** Have a different volunteer read aloud Job 2:8-10. **Job showed amazing faith, didn't he? He used his faith as a shield against everything that Satan threw at him. He could have turned away from God and given up, but instead he kept trusting God, even though he grieved and suffered. Let's talk about how we can be more like Job.**

**Oh, but before we do, let me tell you one thing. This story has a happy ending. God restored Job to even more than he had before! He ended up with a big family and lots of riches.**

ADVENTURES
IN
GROWING

(10 minutes)
## Got God?

This activity can help kids use Job's example of commitment to God to fight their own flaming arrows.

Gather the children into one group.

Say: **Hopefully we won't have to face as many arrows from Satan as Job did. But it's a sure bet that we'll have to face some. So we have to be prepared.**

Ask: • **How did Job defend himself against the trials Satan sent?**

• **How can we defend ourselves against the flaming arrows we face?**

Say: **Job kept his faith no matter what. But that's easier said than done. It takes practice and patience. One way that Job kept his faith when he was tested was to acknowledge that God was in control. Think of three things that God is in control of—things that *only* God can control, like the weather. Turn to someone sitting next to you** and tell the three things you thought of. Then listen while your partner does the same.**

Pause as kids talk. Invite volunteers to share their answers with the rest of the class. Then continue.

Say: **Another way that Job kept his faith in times of trouble was to remember all the good things God had done for him in his life, instead of concentrating just on the bad things. Turn to someone different and tell that person three good things that God has done in your life. Then listen while your partner does the same.** Pause as kids talk. Ask a few volunteers to share their answers with the rest of the class.

**Our faith can be a shield against Satan. It takes courage and strength to hold on to our faith when times are hard. But remember—God will never allow us to be tested beyond what he knows we can handle. He will always be there to help us. And he'll *never* stop loving us. Let's make something to remind us of that.**

**SOUVENIRS** (15 minutes)
## Shield of Faith

This handout can remind kids to hold fast to their faith during times of trouble.

**Items to Pack:** Bibles, copies of the "Shield of Faith" handout (p. 71), colored pencils

Give each child a copy of the "Shield of Faith" handout. Set out colored pencils for kids to share. Give each child a Bible.

Say: **Our faith can be a shield to defend us against whatever Satan throws our way. In each section of your shield, write one situation where your faith might be tested. Maybe you're having trouble making friends and you wonder if God cares. Or maybe someone you love is sick or sad, and you're waiting for God to help. Write a few words to describe the situation, but try to be as specific as possible. Feel free to discuss what you're thinking with someone near you.**

Walk around the room to help kids as needed. If kids have trouble getting started, suggest other scenarios such as being talked about by a friend, or having their parents get divorced.

After kids have written their situations, have them look up the verse at the bottom of each section. Have kids draw a picture of what the verse means to them in the space provided.

Invite volunteers to share what they've written and drawn with the rest of the class. Have kids keep their paper shields in their Travel Journals.

(5 minutes)

Gather kids in a circle on the floor.

Say: **Before we go, let's take time to talk to God. As we saw in the account of Job, God is the only one to turn to in times of trouble. God loves you and cares what happens to you. Silently tell God about a trouble you're facing right now, right this minute.** Pause as kids pray. **Now ask God to help your faith remain strong. Tell him how your faith feels right now and ask him what to do to make it stronger.** Pause as kids pray. **Finally, thank God for being in control, even though times get tough now and then. Thank God for all the good things he's given you in your life, and ask him to remind you of his presence as you go through hard times.**

Close the prayer by asking God to be with each child in class during the coming week, and to strengthen their faith no matter what they may face.

# Shield of Faith

**My faith is tested when**     **My faith is tested when**     **My faith is tested when**

_____    _____    _____

_____    _____    _____

_____    _____    _____

**Read Psalm 3:3, then draw what this verse means to you.**     **Read Psalm 28:7, then draw what this verse means to you.**     **Read Psalm 119:114, then draw what this verse means to you.**

"In addition to all this, take up the shield of faith, with which you can extinguish all the flaming arrows of the evil one" (EPHESIANS 6:16).

# JOURNEY 9

# The Helmet of Salvation

**Pathway Point:** 🌑 We can trust God to protect our thoughts.

**In-Focus Verse:** "Take the helmet of salvation..." (Ephesians 6:17a).

## Travel Itinerary

In today's culture, those who espouse ideologies contrary to God's Word strive to capture children's minds with a wide variety of persuasive techniques. Jesus is different. He places a high priority on our freedom. Jesus never coerces anyone to believe. We come to trust him by experiencing the love and freedom he offers. As we submit to his loving leadership, we find freedom from sin and all that Satan and the world would use to enslave our minds.

Our job is not to load kids down with a lot of man-made rules about what they should and shouldn't think. Instead, use this lesson to help children experience Jesus' love and develop a trusting relationship with him. Then help kids begin to evaluate if their thought life is leading them closer to God or farther from him. Lead them to recognize God's love and wisdom in providing protective armor for our minds—the helmet of salvation.

> **TOUR GUIDE TIP**
>
> The activities in this book have been designed for multi-age groups. Select from the activities, or adapt them as needed for your class.

> **TOUR GUIDE TIP**
>
> Make an overhead transparency of the children wearing armor on page 8. Show this to the children as you talk about the helmet of salvation, and use a colorful marker to highlight the helmets that the children in the picture are wearing.

### DEPARTURE PRAYER

(up to 5 minutes)

Say: **Do you ever think about what you think about? Usually we just...think. And we don't think much about it. Turn to a friend and tell that person the last thing you thought about last night before falling asleep and the first thing you thought about this morning.** Give kids time to share.

**Sometimes we have little control over our thoughts; they just come to us. If I said, "Don't think about pink elephants dancing," what would you most likely think about? Right! Pink elephants dancing!**

**But other times we do choose our thoughts. In school we might think about what our teacher is saying, or instead we might think about what we'll do after school. When we choose a TV show, we are choosing what we'll think about. It's as if our minds have a gate that lets some thoughts in and shuts others out.**

**Fold your hands on top of your head while we pray. When I pray**

about things that you have thought about, open your fingers like a gate and then close them again. If it's not something you think about, keep your fingers closed.

As you pray, allow time between sentences for kids to move their hands.

Pray: **Dear God, Thank you for amazing minds that can think about so many things. Sometimes we think about the beautiful world you've made. Sometimes we think about sharing what we have with others. Other times we think about getting what is best for us. Sometimes we think about doing our best. Other times we think about giving up. Today Lord, help us think about you and learn how your salvation helps protect our thoughts. Amen.**

### (10 minutes)
### Hat Collection

Kids will wear different hats and examine the different thought choices they make.

Place the hats and headgear in the center of the room. As you begin, have each child choose a hat to wear, and have the kids sit in a circle.

Say: **Look around at the different hats. Notice what makes them different and what purposes they serve.**

Ask: • **Which hats keep something out or keep something in?**

• **Which hats serve to identify the people wearing them?**

Say: **Some hats keep things out, such as a winter hat that keeps out cold air. In a bike accident, a helmet keeps your head in one piece! Baseball caps identify the team you're on. I have a special hat, too.** Hold the colander upside down and show it to kids. **See the holes? This hat lets my thoughts out. When I wear this hat, people can hear my thoughts out loud. For example,** (place the colander upside down on your head) **"I think teaching children about Jesus is fun!"** Remove, then replace hat. **"I hope we can go out to eat after church!"** Remove hat. **What thoughts would people know if *you* wore my hat?** Pass the colander around the circle and allow kids to share a thought others might not know about.

**God knows all our thoughts, even without this funny hat. Sometimes our thoughts lead us closer to him. But other times, our thoughts can lead us away from God or cause us to hurt others. Our enemy, Satan, wants us to think about things that will lead us away from God. But** ◖ **we can trust God to protect our thoughts. God**

**Items to Pack:** colander, a variety of hats and headgear

**TOUR GUIDE TIP**
Need some hat tips? See if you can find these for your class: baseball cap, bike helmet, chef's hat, various winter hats, cowboy hat, sombrero, birthday hat, stocking cap, batting helmet, motorcycle helmet, ear muffs, bandanna, firefighter's helmet, straw hats, football helmet... What else can *you* think of?

**FUN FACT**
Some people think the term *ten-gallon hat* means that a cowboy's hat could hold ten gallons of water. Actually, it comes from the Spanish word *galón*, which means "braid." A ten-gallon hat is one with braiding around the brim. The hat itself could probably hold about three quarts.

**SCENIC ROUTE** →

Purchase inexpensive, plain muslin painter caps at a craft store. Have kids use fabric paints or markers to personalize caps. Kids can create pictures or write phrases that will remind them of God's power protecting them with the helmet of salvation.

**Items to Pack:** Bible, large men's clothing (pants, belt, sport coat, shoes, and hat), a briefcase containing several heavy books

**TOUR GUIDE TIP**

Read all of 1 Samuel 17 to understand the context of this story. Be prepared to supplement or correct children's understanding of the climax of the David and Goliath story.

designed spiritual armor to protect us. Ephesians 6:17 says, "Take up the helmet of salvation..." When we have a relationship with Jesus, God gives us the helmet of salvation. It helps us know we're on God's team and protects us from Satan's harmful plans. God's helmet keeps harmful thinking out of our head and loving thoughts in. Let's learn more about God's helmet of salvation.

**STORY EXCURSION**

(15 minutes)

## The Right Armor

Children will provide sound effects and act out the story of David trying on Saul's armor.

Gather the necessary props near where you will tell the story. Tell children you will cue them to provide sound effects during the story. Choose one volunteer to play David and repeat his lines. Have other children help dress David at the appropriate part of the story. Show kids your open Bible, and use the following script to tell the story.

Say: **Our Bible story today comes from 1 Samuel 17. Once there was a boy named David. He was the youngest boy in his family and had seven older brothers. David's job was to watch the sheep.** Cue children to make sheep noises. **While David cared for the sheep, sometimes a lion or bear would scare the flock and steal a sheep.** Cue sound effects. **But David chased the wild animal and rescued the sheep. If the wild animal attacked David, he struck it and killed it. David learned to trust God's protection.**

**David's older brothers served in King Saul's army. One day, David's father gave him supplies and sent him to the Israelite camp to check on his brothers. The Israelites were at war with the Philistines. Goliath, the champion Philistine warrior, stood over nine feet tall. Goliath and the Philistines made fun of the Israelites and of God.**

**How might they have sounded when they made fun of the Israelites?** Cue children for sound effects. **No one wanted to fight Goliath. Each of them pointed at the others and said, "Not me! You go do it!"** Have kids repeat after you.

**David saw the Israelites trembling in fear and heard Goliath making fun of God and the Israelite army. David stood up and said, "I'll fight Goliath!"** Allow David to repeat his line. **King Saul thought David could never fight such a mighty warrior. But David knew God had**

protected him from lions and bears. David knew God would protect him from Goliath, too. So Saul agreed.

To help David get ready to fight, King Saul dressed him in his own armor. Have several kids help dress David in large men's clothing as each item is mentioned. The items should be placed over the child's clothing. He wore the king's pants...the king's belt...the king's coat of armor...the king's boots...the king's helmet...and carried the king's shield. Give the child the briefcase containing books.

Ask: • How do you think David felt under all that armor?

• How would it feel to go through your whole day dressed like this?

• What problems could come from wearing armor that's not made for you?

Say: Saul's heavy armor caused problems for David, too! He was not used to the king's armor. David decided to take it off and fight Goliath without armor—just as he fought the lions and bears. He took only his sling and five smooth stones.

Ask: • How do you think David felt as he got ready to fight Goliath?

• What do you think was going through his mind?

• What thoughts was God protecting him from?

Say: If you've heard this story before, tell what happened in the end.

Allow kids to finish the story, adding details and correcting any misunderstandings.

Ask: • Although David fought Goliath without armor, what protection *did* he have?

• How did David know he could trust God's protection?

• How can we know we will be protected with the armor of God?

Say: David didn't need the king's armor because he trusted God to protect him. God's protection was better for David than the king's finest armor. God's armor is best for us too. When we have a relationship with Jesus, God gives us the helmet of salvation. We know ◗ we can trust God to protect our thoughts.

**FUN FACT**

Bike helmets are 85 percent effective in decreasing the risk of traumatic brain injury. Children ages 11 to 14 are at greatest risk for head injuries because helmet usage is lowest in this age group. Estimates of national usage among child bicyclists range only from 15 to 25 percent.

## Thought Filters

Kids will do a filtering activity and consider what thoughts would lead them closer to God.

Set supplies on the table and gather children around so they can see. Place the colander in one bowl and fill the other with rice. Place the rocks and markers nearby. Have your Bible open to 1 Samuel 17.

Say: **We learned that David trusted God to protect him from Goliath and from fearful thoughts when he was getting ready to fight. We can trust God to protect our thoughts, too. Let's do an activity to see how God's helmet of salvation can help keep harmful thoughts out of our minds while letting good thoughts through. We'll use my funny hat as the filter. The rice will be thoughts that lead us closer to God, and these rocks will be thoughts that might lead us away from God. Think about what goes into your mind as you watch TV, play video games, surf the Internet, or talk with friends.**

Have kids form groups of three or four and discuss the following questions. Have kids report back to the class what their group discovered. Ask:

• **What things come into our minds through TV, music, the computer, friends or other sources, that might lead us away from God?**

• **How can these ideas lead to even more harmful thinking?**

After kids have reported back on their findings, say: **Everyone has thoughts that can lead us away from God. Sometimes kids think about wanting to stay home instead of going to church. Perhaps when you're angry with a friend, you think about how to get back at him or her. You may think about trying to disobey your parents without getting caught.** 🌀 **We can trust God to protect our thoughts from these ideas that can lead to trouble.**

**Choose a thought that sometimes leads you away from God. Select a rock and write that thought on it with a marker.** Give children time to think and write. As children finish, have them mix their rocks into the rice.

**Our minds can be filled with both good and bad thoughts, all mixed together. But when we believe in Jesus and wear the helmet of salvation,** 🌀 **we can trust God to protect our thoughts.**

Let kids take turns scooping the rice and rock mixture into the colander, filtering the rice into the empty bowl until all the rice has been removed. Gather kids in a circle and have them put their hands on the colander and rocks.

Say: **God offers us forgiveness when our thoughts lead us away from him. He helps us get rid of those thoughts...** (remove the colander of rocks from children's view and replace it with the bowl of rice) **...and helps us turn our thoughts toward good things that will draw us closer to him.** Let children wiggle their fingers in the rice for a few moments.

Ask: • **What are things we can think about that would lead us closer to God?**

After hearing their answers, say: **Those are great ideas. The Bible tells us even more good things to think about.** Open your Bible to Philippians 4:8 and read the verse. **We will learn more about these good things God wants us to think about when we make our Souvenirs for our Travel Journals.**

SCENIC ROUTE → Talk about other filters used in everyday life. Kids may be familiar with Internet filters. Parents often use these to keep objectionable material from reaching family members through computer use. Or prepare coffee before class time. Allow the warmer plate and coffee to cool to room temperature. Show kids how the filter works to keep the grounds out but lets the coffee flavor through.

## SOUVENIRS → (10 minutes)
## Hidden in My Helmet

Kids will decorate a helmet with things God encourages us to think about.

Distribute scissors, markers or crayons, and copies of the handout. Have kids cut along the bold lines as marked, then fold the top corners along the dotted lines to create the helmet. Have an older child read the verse at the top of the project.

Say: **This verse describes the types of things God encourages us to think about. Let's brainstorm some things that fit in these categories.** As kids offer ideas, list them on the board or on newsprint. Ask:

• **What are some things that are true?**

• **What are some things that are noble or right?**

Continue to brainstorm ideas for the rest of the verse. When you've completed a list, have kids choose several of these ideas to illustrate beneath the Bible verse inside their helmets.

Ask: • **Of the things we've listed, what are your favorite things to think about?**

• **How can filling your mind with these things protect you from Satan's attacks?**

• **How can thinking about these things help your faith grow?**

Say: **David first learned to trust God's protection from bears and lions, then he grew to trust him when fighting Goliath. When we**

**Items to Pack:** copies of the "Hidden in My Helmet" handout (p. 79), scissors, markers or crayons, newsprint (optional)

TOUR GUIDE TIP Explain any unfamiliar terms to children. *Noble* is likely to be the most difficult for children. You might explain that something noble is of a higher quality and requires more commitment than other things. Serving one's country or working as a missionary in a foreign country could be considered noble callings.

think about these good things, our trust in God grows. Our growing faith helps us remember that  we can trust God to protect our thoughts.

Tell children to put the Hidden in My Helmet projects in the pocket of their Travel Journals.

**Items to Pack:** hats and headgear used in the 1st Stop Discovery

**HOME AGAIN PRAYER** (5 minutes)

Have kids form groups of no more than six. Give one child in each group a hat or helmet. Have children place the hat on the head of the child to their left, then pray for that child to wear God's helmet of salvation and think about things that please God. Kids will continue to pass the hat around the group, praying for each other until everyone has had a turn to pray and be prayed for.

When you notice that groups have finished, conclude with the following:

Pray: **Thank you, God, for giving us the helmet of salvation. Protect our minds from things that would lead us away from you. Help us encourage each other to think about things that will lead us to trust you more. Amen.**

**SCENIC ROUTE** →  Invite an employee of a bicycle shop or a cycling enthusiast to show kids how to properly fit a bike helmet. Help kids see that wearing a helmet is one way of responding to God's loving desire that we be kept safe—in our minds, our spirits, and our bodies, as well.

CUT

FOLD

"Whatever is true, whatever is noble, whatever is right, whatever is pure, whatever is lovely, whatever is admirable— if anything is excellent or praiseworthy—think about such things" (PHILIPPIANS 4:8).

CUT

FOLD

CUT

**Helmet of Salvation**

CUT

CUT

# Hidden in My Helmet

# JOURNEY 10

# The Sword of the Spirit

**Pathway Point:** 🌓 God's Word gives us strength.

**In-Focus Verse:** "Take...the sword of the Spirit, which is the word of God" (Ephesians 6:17b).

## Travel Itinerary

The old saying "Sticks and stones may break my bones, but words will never hurt me" has been proven wrong time and again. Words are powerful. They can hurt, heal, dampen spirits, or encourage the heart.

God's Word is powerful as well. According to 2 Timothy 3:16, the Bible has the power to teach, rebuke, correct, and train in righteousness. God's Word has so much strength that it's referred to as a sword. This journey helps children realize the strength that can be found in the Word of God. When children hide this Word in their hearts, they're defending themselves against attacks and strengthening their faith.

**DEPARTURE PRAYER** (up to 5 minutes)

Gather kids in a circle, then review with them what they've learned so far about the armor of God.

Say: **God wants us to be strong in our faith, and he gives us tools to help us. One of those tools is what the Bible calls the sword of the Spirit, and that's what we'll be talking about today. Before we get started, though, let's pray. Let's ask God to give us strength. Think of an area where you need strength, such as at school, home, with homework, sports, or some other part of your life. I'll begin our prayer, then we'll go around the circle and each person can say the one word they've thought of.** Allow a moment for kids to think of the words they want to say in prayer.

Pray: **Dear Lord, thank you that you give us the tools to fight against what's wrong. Today we want to ask you for strength. Give us strength in these areas** (pause for children to pray). **In Jesus' name, amen.**

**TOUR GUIDE TIP**

The activities in this book have been designed for multi-age groups. Select from the activities, or adapt them as needed for your class.

**TOUR GUIDE TIP**

Make an overhead transparency of the children wearing armor on page 8. Show this to the children as you talk about the sword of the Spirit, and use a colorful marker to highlight the swords that the children in the picture are holding.

**STOP** 1st DISCOVERY (15 minutes)
## A Word
This activity will demonstrate the strength of words.

**Items to Pack:** Bibles

Say: **Words can make us strong, or they can make us weak. I'm going to read a list of words to you. As I say each word, think about how this word makes you feel, or how it would make you feel if someone called you this word. If it makes you feel weak or hurt, slump down or get closer to the floor. If a word makes you feel strong, stand tall and flex your muscles.**

Demonstrate these actions to the kids and have them show you the actions. As you read the following words, pause for a moment after each one to allow children to physically respond.

*Hate*

*Beautiful*

*Love*

*Anger*

*Ugly*

*Important*

*Worthless*

*Special*

*Friend*

*Stupid*

*Smart*

Have children return to their seats. Ask:

• **What are other words that give you strength or that help you feel strong?**

• **Why do you think words can be so powerful?**

Say: **The most important words of all are the words that God gave to us in the Bible. The Bible is like a letter from God to us. The words of the Bible are powerful, and they're not meant to discourage us or hurt us. Instead,** 🌀 **God's Word gives us strength.**

Have kids form pairs, and give each pair a Bible. Have partners read Ephesians 6:17 together.

Ask: • **What is the sword of the Spirit?**

• **Why do you think the Bible calls the Word of God a sword?**

Say: **The Bible says the sword of the Spirit is the Word of God.**

**Maybe that's because a sword is sharp and strong. That certainly describes the Word of God!**

**Items to Pack:** copies of the "You Said It!" script (p. 86)

**STORY EXCURSION**

(15 minutes)
## Standing Before the Sanhedrin

Kids will act out the story of Peter and John before the Sanhedrin to see how the sword of the Spirit gave them strength.

Have kids stay in their pairs, and have partners turn to Acts 4:1-20.

Say: **Right before the action in this story takes place, John and Peter had just healed a crippled man outside the temple. All they had to do was speak and the man was healed! Those were some words of strength! They told everyone who saw what happened that it wasn't their own power that had healed the man; it was the power of Jesus working through them. The Holy Spirit gave them power. Everyone who saw it was amazed, and many people started to believe in Jesus as a result.**

**Well, that didn't sit too well with the rulers. They arrested John and Peter and brought them before the Sanhedrin, which was kind of like a court. Let's find out what happened!**

Give kids several minutes to read the Bible passage in their pairs so they know what happens in the story.

Then choose children to be John, Peter, and the healed man. Have the rest of the class be members of the Sanhedrin. Give each person a copy of the "You Said It!" script and let kids read over their lines. Explain that members of each group will speak their lines in unison, then act out their part of the story. So for example, all members of the Sanhedrin will say their lines together, then act out their part of the story.

Say that since the script is like a rap, you'll need a beat to go with the words. Explain that as each group speak its lines, members of the other groups should quietly make percussion noises to accompany their words. Kids can stomp their feet, slap their thighs, clap their hands, and make drum noises with their mouths. Go quickly through the script once to give kids an idea of how to act out their part of the story and how to make percussion noises while other groups speak. Then have kids perform the script in earnest.

After the performance, lead kids in a round of applause for everyone's participation. Ask:

**SCENIC ROUTE →** For extra fun, videotape the kids' performance. Then have a cast party featuring popcorn and drinks for kids to enjoy as they watch their movie debut.

• **Why do you think the Sanhedrin wanted Peter and John to be quiet?**

• **Why were their words considered so dangerous by the Sanhedrin?**

• **Why do you think Peter and John were able to be so bold before the Sanhedrin?**

Say: **Peter and John knew that it was through the power of Jesus that they had healed the crippled man. They may have been scared when they were arrested and brought before the Sanhedrin. But they told about Jesus boldly and with strength. The Bible tells us that they were filled with the Holy Spirit, and that's why they were able to be so brave and bold. They used the sword of the Spirit to defend themselves in court, and the Holy Spirit gave them the words to say and the courage to say them.**  **God's word gives us strength too. Let's find out more.**

**FUN FACT**

Paul wrote the letter to the Ephesians from prison. Instead of asking the Ephesians to pray for his release, he asked them to pray that he would continue to speak fearlessly about Jesus. Paul knew about the strength of God's Word!

**ADVENTURES IN GROWING**

(10 minutes)
## Strong Swords

Kids will discover ways to use God's Word in their own lives.

Have children return to their pairs. Each pair will need a Bible and a hunk of modeling dough. Assign each pair one of the verses from below, and have the partners read the verse together.

Psalm 119:105

Hebrews 4:12

James 1:22-25

Deuteronomy 8:3

Jeremiah 23:29

**Items to Pack:** Bibles, modeling dough

After pairs have read their verses, say: **Now use your modeling dough to make an object to represent what your verse says about God's Word.**

Allow children a few minutes to work together with their dough. Then have each pair tell what object they made and how this represents God's Word.

Ask: • **How does the item you created give us strength?**

• **How does the item you created help us?**

• **From these examples, what can we learn about God's Word?**

**TOUR GUIDE TIP**

If you have a larger group, assign each passage to more than one pair.

Say:  **God's Word gives us strength. The powerful words God gives us in the Bible help us make good decisions, they help us get closer to God, and they help us know how to treat others. They can encourage us and even be like food to us because they give us strength.**

**Items to Pack:** copies of the "God's Word Is My Sword" handout (p. 85), pens or pencils, scissors, aluminum foil, glue sticks, Bibles

**TOUR GUIDE TIP**
If you have lots of younger kids in class, you may want to write several simple verses, such as Colossians 3:16a and Psalm 119:11a, on a sheet of newsprint for kids to copy.

**SCENIC ROUTE**
This is a great activity for teaching children how to use a concordance. Let children suggest areas where they need strength, such as with gossip, fear, or worrying, and then help kids look these up in a concordance to see what the Bible says about these topics.

**SOUVENIRS** (10 minutes)
# God's Word Is My Sword

Kids will make swords to remind them of the sword of the Spirit and will write encouraging Bibles verses on the swords.

Give each child a copy of the "God's Word Is My Sword" handout. Set out Bibles, pens or pencils, aluminum foil, and glue sticks for kids to use.

Have children cut or tear foil to approximately the size of the sword blade on the handout. Let children glue the foil over the blade to make it look like metal. Then have kids each look up and write a favorite Bible verse on the handle of their swords. Tell kids to choose a verse that will help them have strength in a difficult situation.

When kids have finished writing, let kids share what they wrote with the rest of the class.

Say: **Remember what we talked about in the first activity today? Words have strength and power—and the most powerful words of all are the ones found in the Bible. 🌀 The Bible, God's Word, gives us strength. When you need strength, you can turn to God's Word.**

**HOME AGAIN PRAYER** (10 minutes)

Gather kids in a circle on the floor. Let kids hold the handouts they've worked on.

Say: **Before we close today, let's talk to God. Let's tell him how much we appreciate his Word, and ask him to help us use the sword of the Spirit, the Bible, when we need strength.**

Ask kids to remember the situations they mentioned in the opening prayer. Remind them that they mentioned times or places that they need strength.

In the closing prayer, kids will each repeat their one-word prayer, and then say the verse they wrote on their sword. Go around the circle until each child has prayed. Then close by thanking God for the strength he provides through the Bible.

Have children put their handout in their Travel Journals.

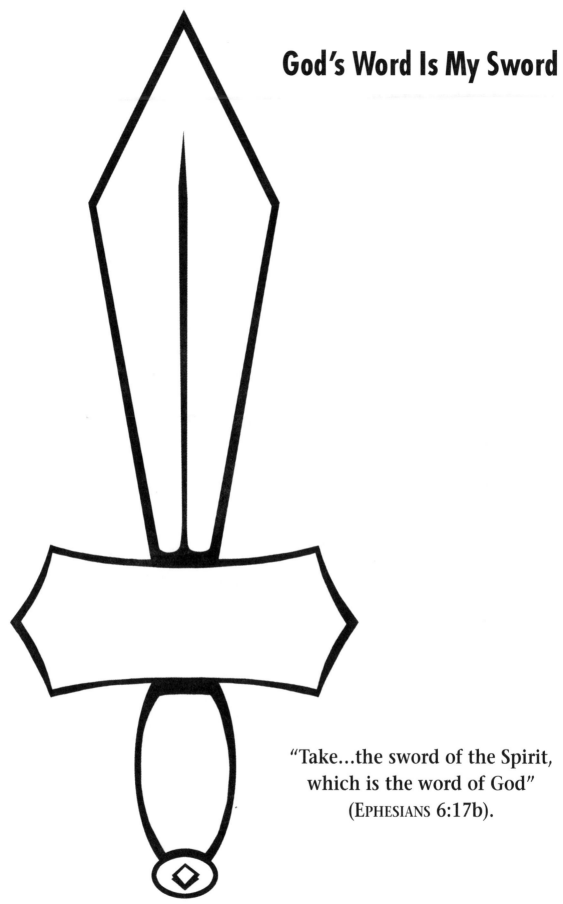

# God's Word Is My Sword

"Take...the sword of the Spirit,
which is the word of God"
(EPHESIANS 6:17b).

# You Said It!

**Sanhedrin:** *(to Peter and John)*

What did you do,

And what did you say?

We just can't have you

Acting that way!

You're under arrest

'Til the morning light.

We're locking you up

Good and tight!

*(Lock up Peter and John.)*

**Peter and John:** *(in jail)*

We don't care

What they may say.

We'll tell about Jesus

Anyway!

**Narrator:**

The very next day

The court did meet.

Peter and John

Were on the hot seat!

**Sanhedrin:** *(to Peter and John)*

Who gave you the strength?

Who gave you the power

To heal a man

In less than an hour?

**Peter and John:** *(to Sanhedrin)*

We tell you the truth.

The man was lame.

And he was healed

By a powerful name.

Whose name, you ask,

And rightly so.

It's the name of Jesus.

Didn't you know?

**Sanhedrin:** *(huddling together)*

We're in trouble,

That's how it goes.

They healed the guy

And everyone knows.

We can't pretend

That the guy can't walk.

So we'll have to make them

Stop this talk.

**Sanhedrin:** *(to Peter and John)*

Don't talk about Jesus

Or mention his name.

We'll be watching,

It's not a game!

**Peter and John:** *(to Sanhedrin)*

Sorry, pals,

That's just not right.

We'll tell about Jesus

With all our might.

We'll be strong,

And we'll be bold.

'Til all the people

Have been told!

Permission to photocopy this handout from *Kids' Travel Guide*™ to the Armor of God granted for local church use.
Copyright © Group Publishing, Inc., P.O. Box 481, Loveland, CO 80539. www.grouppublishing.com

# The Power of Prayer

**Pathway Point:**  Prayer brings us closer to God.

**In-Focus Verse:** "And pray in the Spirit on all occasions with all kinds of prayers and requests. With this in mind, be alert and always keep on praying for all the saints" (Ephesians 6:18).

## Travel Itinerary

Paul's description of the armor of God ends with several verses on prayer, reminding readers that prayer is also useful as a part of God's armor. Through prayer we communicate to God and deepen our relationship with him. Paul tells readers to pray all kinds of prayers and to keep on praying.

While most children understand that prayer is talking to God, many aren't sure what to say to God besides giving him a list of things they want. Use this journey to help children discover that prayer includes praising God, telling him our fears and needs, and sharing our joys and sorrows with him. Most of all, prayer is talking to our truest Friend.

**DEPARTURE PRAYER** (up to 5 minutes)

Ask: • **How many different ways can you think of to communicate?**

Encourage kids to name e-mail, telephone, songs, letters, smoke signals, sign language, and as many other ideas as they can think of.

Ask: • **How do we communicate with God?**

• **Why should we communicate with God?**

Say: **When we communicate with our family and friends, we get to know them better and they get to know us better. It's the same way with God. He wants us to grow close to him, and one way we can do that is to communicate with him. We do this through prayer.** **Prayer brings us closer to God. As we begin our time together today, let's communicate to God with motions.**

Explain that you'll pray out loud. As you pray, children can do any motions they like to act out the words and phrases of your prayer. You may want to pray slowly to give children time to react to the words you say.

**TOUR GUIDE TIP** The activities in this book have been designed for multi-age groups. Select from the activities, or adapt them as needed for your class.

**FUN FACT** United States President Rutherford B. Hayes had the first telephone installed in the White House.

**TOUR GUIDE TIP** Help children be more comfortable expressing themselves in this way by participating in doing motions yourself, and encouraging other adults in the room to do so as well.

Pray: **Dear Lord, we thank you that you hear us, that you love us, and that you want us to be your friends. We praise you because you are awesome and powerful. Help us to listen and learn during our time together today. In Jesus' name, amen.**

### (15 minutes)
### All Kinds of Prayer

Kids will discover a variety of ways to communicate with God.

Say: **After Paul tells us about the pieces of armor in Ephesians 6 he gives some final words to us in verse 18: "And pray in the Spirit on all occasions with all kinds of prayers and requests. With this in mind, be alert and always keep on praying for all the saints."**

**This verse reminds us that we can always talk to God. And when we talk to God, we become closer to him, as we would get closer to a friend. Let's look at some symbols that will help us think about all the ways and places and reasons we can talk to God.**

Have children form four groups. Give each group paper and a pen, then give one group the pencil, one the glasses, one the Bible, and one the shoe.

Say: **Look at your item and brainstorm ideas about what this item might have to do with prayer. Write all your ideas on the paper.**

After several minutes, let each group tell all their ideas. While there are no right or wrong answers, here are some ideas for what each item might represent:

*Shoe:* God hears us no matter where we go, we can ask God for clothing, we can pray while we're walking.

*Pencil:* We can write prayers to God, God hears us at school, we can pray for help on tests.

*Bible:* The Bible has prayers in it, the Bible teaches us about prayer, we can pray Scripture passages.

*Glasses:* We can pray with our eyes open or closed, we can pray for health.

After each group shares, say: **This activity helps us think more about prayer and how important it is. We can pray about anything. We can pray at any time and in any place. We can always talk to God! Prayer isn't listed as a specific piece of armor like the sword or shield, but it's mentioned in the same passage.**

Ask: • **Why do you think prayer is mentioned here with the other pieces of armor?**

• **Is prayer more of a protective piece of armor or a weapon?**

**Items to Pack:** shoe, pencil, Bible, pair of glasses, paper, pens

**TOUR GUIDE TIP**

Let kids know that "the saints" in this verse refers to all Christians.

**TOUR GUIDE TIP**

If you have more than twenty children in your class, form a few extra groups and provide items such as a watch, a coin, a small barbell, and a bar of soap for children to use in their discussions.

**SCENIC ROUTE →**

Use these verses to teach children about different postures of prayer—then try them out!

2 Chronicles 6:13b

Acts 9:40a

Genesis 24:26

I Kings 8:22

Joshua 5:14

Matthew 26:39

**Explain your answer.**

Say: **We know that when we talk to someone we get closer to them and our relationship grows. Prayer can be a part of our spiritual armor because**  **prayer brings us closer to God, who is the greatest protector of all.**

**Items to Pack:** pencils and paper, Bibles

**STORY EXCURSION**

(15 minutes)
## The Lord's Prayer

Kids will explore the example of prayer that Jesus gave in Matthew 6.

Hold up your Bible and say: **The Bible is full of prayers. There are prayers that people prayed asking God for help, prayers asking for healing, prayers of praise telling God how wonderful he is, prayers asking for forgiveness—there are all kinds of prayers in here! We're going to look at one prayer that Jesus prayed. It's called "The Lord's Prayer," and Jesus gave us this prayer as an example of how to pray.**

Help children form five groups. Assign each group one of the following passages. If you have enough children that you need more than five groups, assign one or more of the passages twice.

Matthew 6:9

Matthew 6:10

Matthew 6:11

Matthew 6:12

Matthew 6:13

Have each group read their passage aloud and then rewrite this verse in their own words. Encourage children to choose one or two important words in their verse and to think of other words that have similar meanings. This might help them understand the verse more clearly.

Allow several minutes for groups to work and rewrite their portion of the prayer. Then have each group read both versions of their verse in turn to take a new look at this prayer.

Ask: • **What do the different verses of this prayer suggest that we pray about?**

• **What are the things you're most likely to pray about?**

• **What are things you might want to start adding when you pray?**

• **Why do you think Jesus gave us this example of how to pray?**

• **How can these prayers help us to get closer to God?**

Say: **This passage helps us realize there are a lot of things we can talk to God about! Let's put some of this into practice.**

**Items to Pack:** modeling dough, a globe or world map, photographs of local schools or businesses, mirror, newsprint, markers

ADVENTURES IN GROWING

(15 minutes)
## Prayer Fair

Children will apply what they've learned by praying at various prayer stations.

Set up five stations in your room. You can use tables, or spread a sheet or tablecloth on the floor to designate each station. At Station One place the modeling dough, at Station Two place the globe or map, at Station Three place the photographs, at Station Four place the mirror, and at Station Five place the newsprint and markers.

Say: **We're going to take some time right now to pray. There are five prayer stations set up here. You can go to them in any order, and stay at each one as long as you like. You might have time to get to all of them, or you might only get to two or three. It's up to you because you'll be the one doing the praying at each station.**

Briefly explain what kids should do at each station.

*Station One:* Make the shape of a family member and pray for that person.

*Station Two:* As you look at the map, pray for people in other states and countries. Pray for missionaries in these countries too.

*Station Three:* Choose one or two of the pictures and pray for these local schools and businesses.

*Station Four:* Look into the mirror and pray for yourself.

*Station Five:* Write words of praise to God, telling him what you like about him.

Explain that you expect the room to have a small amount of noise as people move about and talk softly, but that most of the talking should be to God and not to each other. Then allow children to move about the stations as they like. When the time is almost up, announce that children have about a minute to finish at their stations, then they should move back to their seats.

TOUR GUIDE TIP

If you can, have an adult or teen helper at each station to help guide the children.

SCENIC ROUTE →

Add to Station Two by including pictures of missionaries your church supports. Add to Station Three by including pictures of people who serve your community, such as firefighters, nurses, or postal workers.

SCENIC ROUTE →

Create a sixth station by having a qualified adult lead children outside your building and let them pray for what they see. They might pray for nearby families or businesses or thank God for what they see in nature.

**SOUVENIRS** (10 minutes)

### Prayer Path

Children will see how they can move closer to God through prayer.

**Items to Pack:** copies of the "My Prayer Path" handout (p. 92), crayons or markers, pencils

Give each child a copy of the "My Prayer Path" handout, and make pencils and crayons or markers available.

Explain that children will write a short prayer in each section of the path. Remind children that prayers can be for things they need, for other people, words of praise to God, or prayers of thanks. Encourage children to include a variety of prayers along their path. Children who do not write can draw pictures of things they'd like to pray about or that they're thankful for.

Allow children time to work, then say: **This picture helps us remember that** ⏾ **prayer brings us closer to God. When we talk to God and spend time with him, our friendship with God gets stronger. As you pray the prayers you've written, you can move your fingers along the path to represent moving closer to God.**

**HOME AGAIN PRAYER** (5 minutes)

Have children form pairs, keeping their handouts from the previous activity with them.

Say: **With your partner, take turns praying the prayers on your Prayer Path. Start with the person who is the tallest. That person will pray what's on the first step of the path, then the other person will pray what's on his or her first step. Continue going back and forth until each of you has told God all the prayers on your path.**

Allow a few minutes for children to do this, then close by praying: **Lord, we thank you that we can come to you at any time and no matter where we are. Thank you that you love us enough to want to listen to us and be close to us. Help us to put you first in our lives and share everything with you. In Jesus' name, amen.**

Have children put their handouts into their Travel Journals.

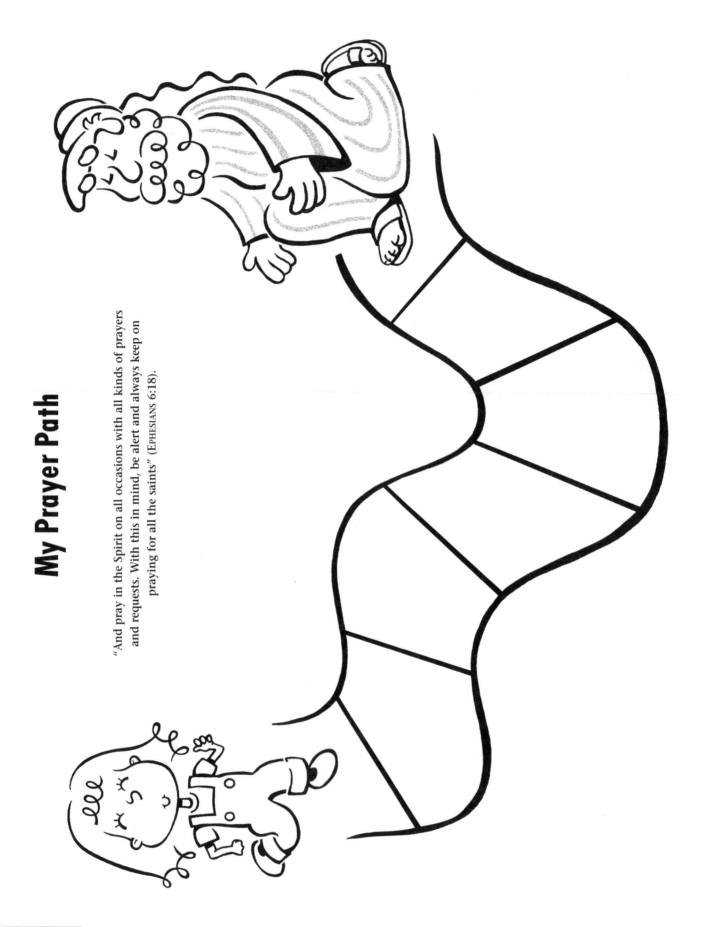

# My Prayer Path

"And pray in the Spirit on all occasions with all kinds of prayers and requests. With this in mind, be alert and always keep on praying for all the saints" (EPHESIANS 6:18).

# JOURNEY 12

# Stand Firm With Family and Friends

**Pathway Point:**  God gives us help to stand firm.

**In-Focus Verse:** "Therefore, my dear brothers, stand firm. Let nothing move you" (1 Corinthians 15:58a).

## Travel Itinerary

Ecclesiastes 4:12 says, "Though one may be overpowered, two can defend themselves. A cord of three strands is not quickly broken." This verse reminds us that it's difficult for one person to stand alone against the pressures of life. But when two or three stand together, there's strength.

A soldier is rarely sent alone into battle, and the same is true for those engaged in spiritual battles. There's strength in numbers. This journey helps children see that their friends and families can be the ones to help them stand firm as they face the battles ahead of them. Use this lesson to help children turn to those who can help them make wise choices and who can stand with them against the attacks of the enemy.

**TOUR GUIDE TIP**

The activities in this book have been designed for multi-age groups. Select from the activities, or adapt them as needed for your class.

**DEPARTURE PRAYER** (up to 5 minutes)

Have children form pairs. Encourage kids to find partners who are about the same height. Have partners face each other, extend their arms, and join hands as if they were going to form a bridge. Tell partners to lean toward each other and to balance by pushing against the hands of their partner. Have children take one or two steps away from each other while still leaning in, to see that they can still stand by holding each other up.

Say: **While you're standing like this, holding each other up, pray for each other. Ask God to help your partner stand firmly with God.**

Allow a minute for children to pray short prayers,

**SCENIC ROUTE →**

Use large blank index cards and markers to make cards for church "family members." Ask children to make cards of encouragement for those who might not expect to receive one. Explain that since we're all part of God's family, we need to encourage each other and show each other support. Be sure to mail the cards after class.

**TOUR GUIDE TIP**

Some children may be struggling with difficulties at home, or may be from homes that are not spiritually supportive. Be sensitive to these children and their needs. This may be your opportunity to model that you will stand firm with that child.

93

then pray: **Heavenly Father, we thank you for our families and friends. We're glad that we have each other to help us stand firm in our faith. Help us to remember to pray for our friends and family every day. God, teach us what it means to be part of your family and how to act like your family. As we stand firm with our family and friends, help us let others know that we do this because we are all part of your family. Amen.**

**Item to Pack:** masking tape

### 1st STOP DISCOVERY — Friend Tag (10 minutes)

This game illustrates the need to stand firm with family and friends.

Place tape across two ends of your playing area, as shown. Form two teams, and have each team stand behind one of the boundaries.

Explain that kids on Team A will turn their backs while Team B sneaks up behind them. When you clap your hands, kids on Team A will turn around and try to tag those on Team B. Those who are tagged will become part of Team A. Kids on Team B may avoid being tagged by running back behind their own boundary line, or by quickly grabbing hands with another person from Team B and standing firm together.

Play the game several times, having teams take turns sneaking up on the other team. Remind kids that they cannot grab hands with a partner until after you clap your hands. After playing several rounds, have children return to their seats. Ask:

• **Was it easier to run back or to stand still with a partner? Why?**

• **When do friends or family members make life seem easier?**

• **What are times you'd like to have a friend or family member nearby to help you stand firm?**

Say: **Sometimes it may seem best to run or retreat from our problems, but God wants us to face our problems. It is easier to stand firm when we have support from our family and friends. We give our family and friends support so that they can stand firm too. Through our family and friends,** ◐ **God gives us help to stand firm.**

**TOUR GUIDE TIP** Today's children are used to thinking of themselves as part of larger families due to stepfamilies and different living arrangements. Affirm that each family is special, no matter how big or small.

94

(10 minutes)
## Firm Against Foes

Kids will work together as they hear the Bible story.

**Items to Pack:**
1 piece of construction paper per child

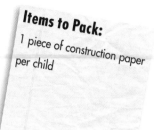

Give every child one piece of construction paper. Have children stand in one large circle, facing in toward the center of the circle. Then have every other child in the circle turn and face the opposite direction so that one child faces in, the next faces out, the next faces in, and so on. Then have each child take one large step backward. This will leave children facing each other with gaps between them on all sides. Explain that kids are now in battle formation. Stand outside the circle.

Say: **We are going to practice standing firm with our family and friends like two brothers from the Bible. Their names were Joab and Abishai. While I tell this account from the Bible, I am going to be walking around your battle formation. I'll try to get through your lines as many times as I can. You can only stop me by holding your shields up to cover the spaces where I try to get in. You must help the people all around you There are a lot of spaces for me to get in, so I want you to work together to keep me out.** Have the children practice as you feint going in once or twice before the story begins. Throughout the story, keep moving around the circle, trying to get inside before children can block you. If you get inside, keep moving around as you read and try to get out. Keep moving in, around, and out as children block.

This account is from 2 Samuel 10:9-14. Joab was a commander in king David's army. David sent Joab and Joab's brother, Abishai, to lead an army against the Ammonites because the Ammonites had mistreated some people from Israel. When the Ammonites realized the army of Israel was coming, they hired the Arameans to come fight with them. Can you keep all these armies straight?

Joab saw that the Ammonites were on one side of the Israelite army and the Arameans were on the other side of his army. The soldiers in the Israelite army were in trouble because they were surrounded!

Joab divided the army in two and led the some of the best fighters against the Arameans. He put his brother, Abishai, in charge of the other soldiers to fight against the Ammonites. Joab told his brother that if the Arameans were too strong, Abishai should bring his soldiers to rescue Joab. Joab promised Abishai that if the Ammonites were too strong, then he would come rescue Abishai. They would help each other in battle.

These brothers were strong because they were going to stand firm together. Best of all, Joab didn't forget about God during the battle! He told Abishai to "be strong and fight bravely for our people and the cities of our God." Joab reminded Abishai that God would do "what was good in his sight."

An amazing thing happened during the battle! When Joab's troops started beating the Arameans, the Ammonites fighting Abishai's troops decided to run away too! God had helped both brothers because they stood firm together!

Let's wave our shields back and forth in the air in a victory celebration! After kids have done this, ask them to sit down and put away their papers. Then ask:

• **What does the saying "I've got your back" mean?**

• **How is that saying like what happened in our Bible story?**

• **What can we learn about working together from this Bible story?**

• **First Corinthians 15:58a says, "Therefore, my dear brothers, stand firm. Let nothing move you." How were Joab and Abishai living out that Bible verse?**

• **How can we live out that Bible verse?**

Say: **Just as you stood together against me during our story, Joab and Abishai stood firm together against an opponent too. They were there to help each other when help was needed. We can learn from their example how to stand firm together. Although we aren't fighting together in a traditional battle, we stand firm by being there for our family and friends. Taking time to help with chores, calling a friend who needs us, or offering a seat to someone on the bus are ways that we strengthen our relationships with our family and friends. Through our families and friends,**  **God gives us help to stand firm.**

**Items to Pack:** craft sticks, pencils, Bible

---

### ADVENTURES IN GROWING

(10 minutes)
## Not Easily Broken

Children will experiment to see how standing together helps make them stronger.

Give each child a craft stick and a pencil. Have kids write their own names on their sticks and then think of one thing that makes life hard for them. This might be schoolwork, kids who make fun of them, problems at home, worries, and so on. Say: **Your stick will represent you. As you think of your problem, break your stick in half.**

Ask: • **Was it easy or hard to break the stick?**

Say: **The stick was easily broken when it was alone. This reminds me of a Bible verse.** Have a child read Ecclesiastes 4:12 aloud. Ask:

• **What does this verse have to do with our experiment?**

Give children more craft sticks to write their own names on, then have them form groups of five. Have one child in each group share the problem he or she was thinking of. Then have each child in the group hand his or her craft stick to the child who shared and say, "I'll stand with you." Then have the child who shared put all the craft sticks into one stack and try to break them. Most children will not be able to break this many sticks at once.

Ask: • **Why did it get harder to break the sticks?**

• **How does being with our friends and family make us stronger?**

• **How would having friends and family members standing with you help you stand firm against your specific problem?**

• **Who can you stand with against his or her problem?**

Say: **Like the sticks, we need to stand firm with our families and friends so that nothing can move us or break us away from our faith.**

### SCENIC ROUTE →

Before class, make rice cereal and marshmallow snacks, and use a small gingerbread-man cookie cutter to cut out a figure for each child.

Have kids connect their cereal figure's sticky arm to the arm of another cereal figure. Ask them to carefully pull them apart and then reattach their figure to a different friend's cereal figure. Ask them to carefully pull these figures apart too. As kids eat their treats, remind them that friends and family stick together and that we all can stand firm in our faith because we're not alone.

We need to share with others the fact that God will help us. God has given us each other so that no one has to stand alone.

**Items to Pack:** copies of the "Standing Firm" handout (p. 100), markers or crayons, two large books (such as Bibles or dictionaries), an empty soda can

**TOUR GUIDE TIP**

Have several books and empty soda cans available so more children can participate in the experiment at once.

**SOUVENIRS** (10 minutes)
## Standing Firm

Children will see how others can help them stand firm.

Say: **We're going to do an experiment with our Souvenir today.** Give each child a copy of the handout and make markers or crayons available. **Turn the paper to the blank side and draw a quick picture of yourself.** Give kids a few moments to complete this task, then take the paper of one child to use as a demonstration.

Place two books on a table or where all the children can see them. Lay them about six inches apart. Place the paper with the child's picture facing up across the two books. It may sag a tiny bit in the middle, but it will stay. Say: **Alone, this person is doing pretty well...until a big problem comes along!** Stand the empty soda can on the paper. The paper will collapse under the weight. **It looks like this person needs some help!**

Have kids turn their papers to the side with the dotted lines. Tell kids to write the names of friends or family members who can help them stand strong in their faith in the blank spaces between lines. Then have children accordion-fold their papers along the dotted lines.

Choose another child's paper to use for demonstration. Place the accordion-folded paper across the two books, with the names of friends and family members facing up. Say to the child: **You have a lot of people standing firm with you! Let's see what happens when problems come your way.** Stand the empty soda can on the folded paper. It will hold up against the weight.

As time permits, let the rest of the children participate in this experiment.

Ask: • **Why did the paper hold the can the second time we tried this experiment?**

• **Why did the folds in the paper make the people appear to stand closer together?**

• **Who can you stand firm with this week?**

Have children place their papers in their Travel Journals.

**HOME AGAIN PRAYER**

(5 minutes)

Have children stand in a large circle and link elbows. Crowd together so that everyone is pressing against each other on both sides.

Say: **Let's stand firm together as we pray.**

Pray: **Father, we know that you give us family and friends to help us stand firm in our faith. Thank you for giving us each other. Let us stand firm for each other so that our family and friends will have the courage to stand firm in their faith too. Amen.**

# Standing Firm

"Therefore, my dear brothers, stand firm. Let nothing move you"
(1 CORINTHIANS 15:58a).

# Standing Firm in the World

**Pathway Point:**  We can stand firm with God every day.

**In-Focus Verse:** "Therefore, my dear brothers, stand firm. Let nothing move you. Always give yourselves fully to the work of the Lord, because you know that your labor in the Lord is not in vain" (1 Corinthians 15:58).

## Travel Itinerary

Every Christian has trouble standing firm when tough times, discouragement and peer pressure hit. And children are certainly no exception. In fact, children are now exposed to more temptation than ever before. Advertising on television tempts kids to become voracious consumers. Cable television and computer games tempt kids with immoral images and messages. Kids are encouraged to emulate sports heroes, rock musicians, and movie stars who do not promote age-appropriate lifestyles or messages. Kids need help to stand up to the pressures of the media and make good choices.

The good news is that the Bible tells us in Ephesians 6 that we can stand firm for God no matter what comes our way. In fact, Paul writes that the reason we put on the full armor of God is so that we can stand firm when the day of evil comes. Isn't it great to know that God gives us everything we need to serve him!

Use this lesson to help kids learn that we can stand firm for God every day.

> **TOUR GUIDE TIP** The activities in this book have been designed for multi-age groups. Select from the activities, or adapt them as needed for your class.

> **TOUR GUIDE TIP** Don't forget that children face very real problems as they seek to serve Jesus in their daily lives. Pray that you'll be especially sensitive to children who are facing difficulties serving God. Be ready to encourage and pray with children individually.

**DEPARTURE PRAYER** (5 minutes)

Welcome the children and have them sit on the floor.

Say: **We're learning to wear the armor of God and stand firm against things that would lead us away from a relationship with God.**

Ask: • **How do people try to get kids your age to turn away from God?**

• **How do some movies, songs, games, or other activities try to get you to turn away from God?**

• **How do you feel about these people or things?**

Say: **All of us face challenges to our faith. God wants us to be close to him and to always be growing in our relationship with him, and** that's why he's provided the armor of God—so we can stand firm in our relationship with God. Let's begin our time together by asking God to help us stand firm.

Have the children keep their eyes open as they join you in the motions used in your prayer.

Pray: **Dear God, sometimes we get so discouraged** (slump your shoulders). **We face tough times** (hang your head), **we get sad** (wipe tears from your eyes), **and we feel like we just can't win** (slump your shoulders again). **It can be hard to be a Christian because so many people aren't Christians and they don't understand us. Sometimes they even make fun of us. But God, you've given us a great set of armor to wear.** Pretend to put on a set of armor. **You've given us everything we need to stand firm for you every day** (stand up tall and proud). **Thank you, God, for helping us learn about your armor** (look up to God). **Today, please help us learn how to use your armor to serve you** (bow before God). **In Jesus' name, amen.**

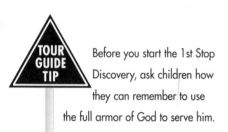

Before you start the 1st Stop Discovery, ask children how they can remember to use the full armor of God to serve him.

(10 minutes)
## Blown Away

Children will compare physically standing firm to standing firm in their faith.

Say: **Today we're going to talk about standing firm. We talked last time about how family and friends can help us stand firm. Today we're going to think about how 🌙 we can stand firm with God every day. This means standing firm against the pressures of our world—against those who tell us it's foolish to have faith in God. We'll start with a fun activity.**

**Let's all stand on our tiptoes and walk around the room. When I say "slow," walk slowly. When I say "fast," walk quickly. When I say "stop," stop immediately. Ready? Let's go.**

Walk with the children on your tiptoes around the room. Periodically call out "slow," "fast" or "stop," and have the children follow your directions. After a couple of minutes, have the children stop.

Ask: • **Was it easy or hard to keep your balance while walking on your tiptoes? Explain.**

Say: **Now let's all stand on one leg. Follow my directions. Ready? Let's go.**

Balance on one leg with the children as you call out these directions. Pause for about ten seconds after each direction.

**Look up.**

**Look down.**

**Lean forward.**

**Lean backward.**

**Hop.**

**Stand still.**

**Switch legs.**

**Switch legs again.**

**Close your eyes.**

**Stand still.**

**Take a seat on the floor.**

Ask: • **Was it easy or hard to keep your balance while standing on one leg? Explain.**

• **Did you ever think you were going to fall?**

• **How did that make you feel?**

Say: **Now I'd like for you all to stand up and show me how you could stand firm so you'd keep your balance and wouldn't fall over.**

Have the children stand up and stand firm. Go around the room and *gently* shake each child's shoulder to test how firm they're standing. Say things like, "You're standing really firm!" or "I don't think even a hurricane could knock you over!"

Have the children sit on the floor again.

Say: **The Bible talks a lot about how important it is to stand firm. But the Bible isn't talking about standing firm on your feet like we were doing.**

Ask: • **What do you think the Bible means when it says to stand firm?**

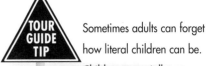

**STORY EXCURSION**

(15 minutes)
## Nehemiah's Wall

Children will act out the story of Nehemiah to see how to stand firm for God.

Show children your Bible and open it to the book of Nehemiah. Tell children you're going to share with them the true story of what happened to Nehemiah.

Choose one child to be Nehemiah. Have everyone else sit on the floor—they

**Item to Pack:** Bible

are the stones. Read aloud the following script and have Nehemiah and the stones act it out.

Say: **This is the story of a man named Nehemiah. This story comes from the Bible. Nehemiah lived thousands of years ago. He was a Jewish man, but he didn't live in Israel. That's because the country of Babylon had won a war against Israel and many of the Jews were taken to Babylon to live.**

**One day some people from Israel came and gave Nehemiah bad news. Nehemiah, look like you've just been given bad news.** (Pause.) **The people said that the protective wall around Jerusalem was in ruins. That meant that Jerusalem was unprotected. Its enemies could easily attack the city. Also, Jerusalem was a very special city to the Jews. It was their homeland. And it was land that God had given them. To hear that the wall was in ruins made Nehemiah feel much the same as you would feel if you heard your home had been destroyed. Everyone show me how your face would look if you'd just found out your home had been destroyed.** (Pause.)

**This made Nehemiah terribly sad. Nehemiah, look sad.** (Pause.) **He cried,** (pause) **he mourned** (pause)**, he fasted** (pause)**, he prayed** (pause)**. Finally he came up with a plan. He asked his boss, the king, to let him go to Jerusalem and rebuild the walls. The king gave him permission, so he traveled to Jerusalem. Nehemiah, you can walk around the room once to show you've been traveling.** (Pause.)

**When Nehemiah got there, he inspected the wall and found there was much work to be done. The wall was in terrible shape. So he got to work. He organized the people and they all started to rebuild the wall with stones. The stones were very heavy. It was hot and dusty work.**

Have Nehemiah start building the wall by taking another child by the hand and leading him or her to the front of the room. Have Nehemiah take another child and lead him or her to stand next to the first child. Have Nehemiah link their elbows together so that a circular wall is begun. After Nehemiah has used about half of the "stones," have him pause.

Say: **The work was very hard. And two men made it even harder to get the work done. Sanballat and Tobiah discouraged the workers by teasing them. They even came up with a plan to fight against the workers and stir up trouble.**

**SCENIC ROUTE →** Gather enough LEGO blocks and building blocks to let children work in small groups to build the wall around Jerusalem while you tell this story. Be sure to have enough LEGO people for each group to have a Nehemiah, a Sanballat, and a Tobiah, as well as workers.

Have two volunteers pretend to be Sanballat and Tobiah and walk around the room, threatening to tear down the wall.

Say: **The Bible doesn't tell us exactly why Sanballat and Tobiah were so mean. But some think that they had become important people in the area. Nehemiah was moving in on their turf, and that made them mad.**

**But Nehemiah stood firm against the threats. He was determined to finish the task. He posted guards along the wall to watch for Sanballat and Tobiah. The people who worked carried weapons with them just in case there was an attack. They stood firm too. And they all worked from the time the sun came up to the time the sun went down. The Bible says they worked with all their heart.**

**Nehemiah, let's finish the wall.** Have Nehemiah continue to put "stones" into place until there is a complete wall in the shape of a circle that uses all the children.

**Fifty-two days after it was begun, the wall was finished. Nehemiah and the people of Jerusalem stood firm and completed their task even though Sanballat and Tobiah had teased them, discouraged them, and planned to attack them. Good job, everyone! Thanks for helping tell the Bible story today.**

Have the children sit down right where they are. Have the children who played the three characters join the group.

Ask: • **What made it hard for Nehemiah and the people of Jerusalem to stand firm?**

• **When have you faced tough times like that, when it was hard to stand firm for God?**

• **What did you do?**

• **How can the armor of God help us to ◑ stand firm for God every day?**

• **The Bible tells us that Nehemiah posted guards around the wall while they were building. Do you think you could have "guards" in your life to help you stand firm?**

• **Who do you know that would be a good guard in your life to help you stand firm?**

Say: **All of us face times when it's tough to stand firm for God. That's why God has given us the full armor of God. We have the belt of truth, the breastplate of righteousness, our feet fitted with readiness,**

**FUN FACT**

The Bible even says that they worked so hard they didn't take the time to change their clothes—for nearly two whole months! Yuck! Do you think they at least washed their hands?

the shield of faith, the helmet of salvation, the sword of the Spirit, and prayer—all to help us stand firm for God. Even when it's hard, we can ask God for help. Right now, let's stand up and join hands and say, ◑ "We can stand firm for God every day."

Have everyone stand up in the circle, join hands and say, "We can stand firm for God every day."

ADVENTURES IN GROWING

(15 minutes)
## Firm Responses

Children will create skits to role-play standing firm.

Have all the children stand in the wall formation that they made during the Story Excursion.

Say: **You guys make a great wall. You look strong! I'm sure that you'd do a great job at protecting the city of Jerusalem.**

**Did you know that the Bible talks about how Christians are a strong structure? It doesn't say that Christians are like a wall, but it does say that Christians are like a strong building. I'd like for you to reorganize yourselves into a strong building shape.**

Give the class a few minutes to create a building shape. This could be as simple as forming a square instead of a circle. Encourage the children and give them guidance as needed. When the children have formed a building shape, gently try to break through. Make a big show of this, but be sure that you aren't successful.

Say: **Stand there and pretend to be a building while I read you the passage from the Bible.**

**"And now you have become living building-stones for God's use in building his house. What's more, you are his holy priests; so come to him—[you who are acceptable to him because of Jesus Christ]—and offer to God those things that please him"** (1 Peter 2:5, The Living Bible).

**Wow! Isn't that great? We're the stones that God's using to build his house. We can be like strong stones. ◑ We can stand firm with God every day. And we can offer to God those things that please him. Let's talk about how to stand firm and please God.**

Help the children form pairs. Be sure to put younger children with older children. And be sure there's at least one strong reader in each pair.

Say: **In just a moment, I'll give you a slip of paper. Read the paper and talk about how you would stand firm in the situation you've been given. Then together come up with a short skit to show how** you would stand firm in that situation. You've got five minutes to work.

Give the children five minutes to talk about their situations and come up with a short skit. Wander around the room, giving help and advice to any of the pairs that need it.

After five minutes, call time. Have each pair present their skit to one of the other pairs. Then have children return to their seats.

Ask • **Was it hard to come up with ways to stand firm for God in the situations you had? Why or why not?**

Have children discuss the following questions with their partners:

• **What situations do you face in your life where you need to stand firm for God?**

• **What can you do to stand firm in that situation?**

After a couple of minutes, invite volunteers to share their ideas with the class.

Say: **The Bible tells us that when we put on the full armor of God, we will be prepared to stand firm. Listen to what the Bible says.**

**"Therefore put on the full armor of God, so that when the day of evil comes, you may be able to stand your ground, and after you have done everything, to stand" (Ephesians 6:13).**

**With God's armor, we'll be able to stand up against evil. That's great news! Let's think more about that as we work on our Travel Journals.**

If time permits, you can have all the pairs perform their skits for the entire group.

**SOUVENIRS** (10 minutes)

## Bricks in the Wall

Children will complete their Travel Journals with a reminder to stand firm.

**Items to Pack:** copies of "Bricks in the Wall" handout (p. 110), crayons or markers

Give children the handouts and drawing supplies. Have them think of a situation they'd face in each of the locations shown that would require them to stand firm. Have them draw themselves standing firm in the locations that are shown on each brick of the handout. Then help the children find partners. Have the children in each pair tell each other about the situations they drew on their papers.

Say: **No matter what we face in our lives,**  **we can stand firm with God every day. Nehemiah reminded us how important it is to stand up to bullies or other distracting influences and to keep working hard even when the job is really hard. Nehemiah stood firm and accomplished great things for God. You can do great things for God too.**

**SCENIC ROUTE** You may want to create a standing-firm wall in your classroom. Cut bricks from red construction paper and have kids draw pictures of how they stand firm for God in their daily lives. Invite the children to attach the bricks to the wall with wall putty.

**SCENIC ROUTE →** If time allows, let children look through their Travel Journals to see all they've learned about the armor of God in the past weeks.

Have children put these pages into their Travel Journals, and remind them to take their journals home with them at the end of class today.

**HOME AGAIN PRAYER** (5 minutes)

Say: **We've learned a lot about the armor of God over the past weeks. Let's put on the full armor of God so that we can stand our ground.**

As you read each part of the armor, lead children in pantomiming putting on that item.

**We want to buckle the belt of truth around our waists.** (Buckle a belt around your waist.)

**And we'll put the breastplate of righteousness in place.** (Put on a breastplate.)

**We will fit our feet with the readiness that comes from the gospel of peace.** (Put on shoes.)

**And we'll take up the shield of faith.** (Pick up a shield and hold it in front of you.)

**Also, we'll put on the helmet of salvation.** (Put on a helmet.)

**And the sword of the Spirit, which is the Word of God.** (Pick up a sword and wave it around.)

**Now that we've put on the armor of God, let's pray together. Listen to what I pray. Every time I say "stand firm," stomp your feet as hard as you can and call out, "Stand firm," in a strong voice.**

Pray: **Here we are, God, dressed in the full armor of God. We're ready to serve you every day. At church we will stand firm** (children stomp and say "stand firm"). **At home we will stand firm** (children stomp and say "stand firm"). **At the playground we will stand firm** (children stomp and say "stand firm"). **At school, in sports, in all our activities, we will stand firm** (children stomp and say "stand firm"). **No matter where we go, we will stand firm** (children stomp and say "stand firm"). **In Jesus' name, amen.**

# Stand Firm Situations

**Chris:** The most popular kid in school wants you to come over and play video games. You know that your parents don't approve of this person's video games and wouldn't want you to play. What do you do, and what do you tell the popular friend?

**Pat:** You've been watching music videos a lot and you really like one group. When your grandparents send you birthday money you go to the mall and you see an outfit that looks just like what the lead singer wears. You know your parents wouldn't approve of the outfit, but it's your money. What would you do, and what would you say to your parent about it?

**Sydney:** All of the big kids at your school have started using a word that's kind of rude. You really want to fit in with the kids at school, and if you're going to be cool, you've got to start saying that word. What do you decide to do, and what do you say to your best friend about it?

**Sam:** The coolest new toy is an action figure from a new television show. The show is really violent. The toy says lots of things about hurting others and destroying things. Everyone at school thinks the show and the toy are really great. What do you do, and what do you say to a schoolmate who just bought the new toy?

"Therefore, my dear brothers, stand firm. Let nothing move you. Always give yourselves fully to the work of the Lord, because you know that your labor in the Lord is not in vain" (1 CORINTHIANS 15:58).

## Bricks in the Wall